I0759400

Sophie-May Williams

Sabrina Carpenter

The Ultimate Unofficial Short 'n' Sweet Fanbook

HarperCollins*Publishers*

This work has not been officially endorsed by Sabrina Carpenter but pays homage to the phenomenally talented icon that she is. Written by a fan, for fans, this is a love letter to Sabrina for all those she inspires.

Contents

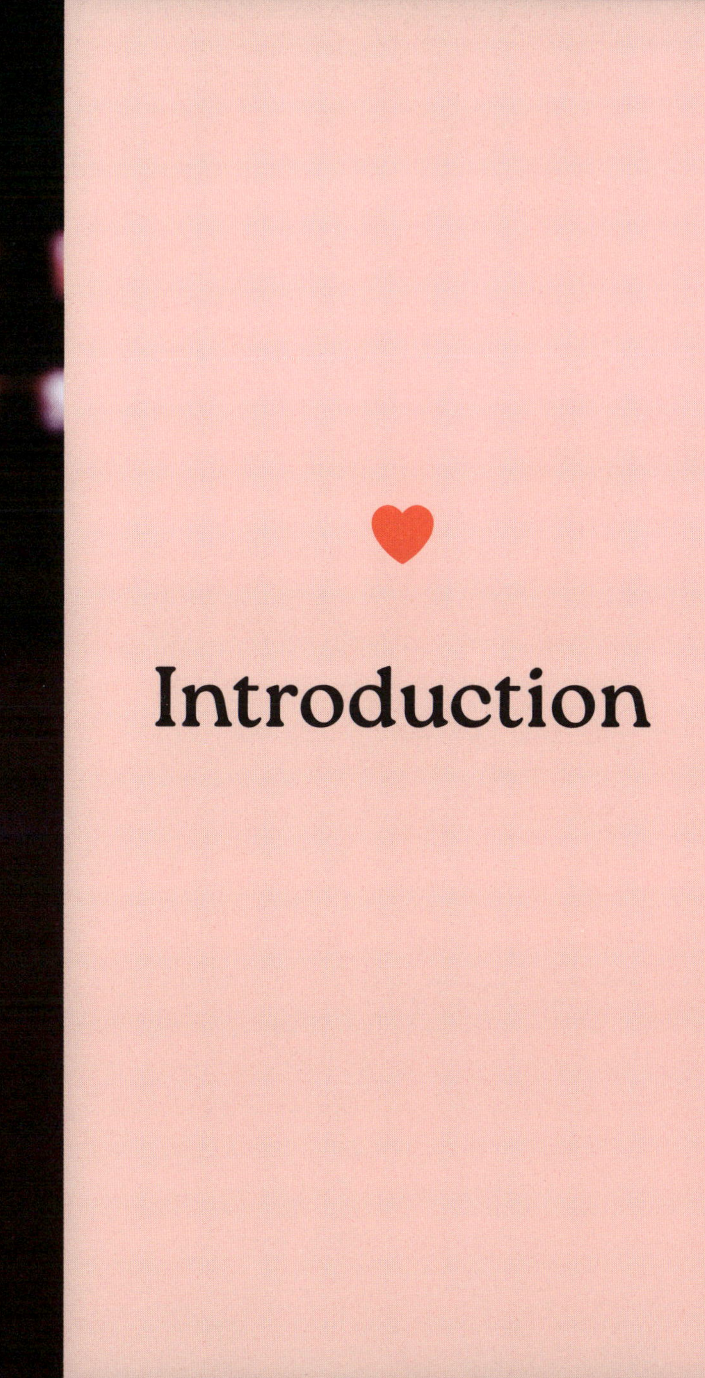

Introduction

Sabrina Carpenter is the Gen Z pop queen. Born in 1999, in Pennsylvania, Sabrina always knew entertainment would be the path she would follow.

She told *Paper* magazine in 2024: 'I don't know how to describe it. When you're a child and you just have a feeling of, I know I'm going to do this someday. I know I'm going to do this for the rest of my life. I know this is the path I need to follow, whatever that means for me, and whatever success that means for me is what I'm destined for.'

Little did Sabrina know what kind of success she would accomplish. Or that she'd one day embark on stratospheric pop domination, with no signs of slowing down so far ...

Get out your musical encyclopedias, because we're taking a trip down memory lane. In the 80s we had Madonna. In the 90s it was all about Britney Spears. In the noughties, Taylor Swift wore the millennial crown. My point? In every generation an artist comes along who defines their era. They are the poster child of the genre. The benchmark for success. The name on everyone's lips. Right now, it's Sabrina Carpenter's world, and we are all living in it.

So, how does a small-town girl from Quakertown, Pennsylvania, go from obscurity to pop powerhouse, you ask? According to Sabrina, as cliché as it sounds, it's all about ambition, staying true to and believing in yourself. Even in the face of adversity. But most importantly? Maintaining the notion that success is not as important as the love you have for your art. If it's meant to be, the rewards will follow.

As we all know, Sabrina is at one with self-deprecating humour. When reminiscing on her 'journey' to the top of the music industry, she likens her story to the tortoise in the folklore fable 'The Tortoise and the Hare'. While accepting the *Variety* Hitmakers Rising Artist Award in December 2023, she recalled: 'Something that my mom always said to me as a little girl that really annoyed me was that I am the tortoise … throughout my life, [I was] being told, "Sabrina, you're the tortoise, just chill." In moments of frustration and confusion it can feel like a letdown, but it turns out it's actually a very good thing.'

We can all agree that Sabrina's back catalogue of competitions, teenage tweets dreaming of world tours and being too young to enter karaoke contests now feel like full-circle moments; all important segments of her inevitable rise to fame, no matter how big or small.

Case in point: Sabrina placing third in a singing competition in 2009, backed by then-Disney sweetheart Miley Cyrus, cemented her fate as a future Disney darling and pop princess. Following that near-win, Hollywood Records caught wind of the young aspirational singer and later signed a five-album deal with her, aged 12. Whether the label had the ability to predict the next 15 years and could later claim to have soft-launched a star is debatable. What's *not* up for debate is Sabrina proving that the journey of life is not about winning, but about seizing the opportunities and experiences wherever we find them.

Take away all the glitz and glamour, and at the crux of the Sabrina Carpenter brand she's still the same little girl who fell in love with entertaining and finds joy in sharing that passion with the world.

It's perhaps why she's so easy to relate to. If Sabrina can work hard, believe in herself and achieve her wildest dreams, so can we. Still dreaming to this day, she proves that it's never too late for us to follow our hearts.

Ultimately, Sabrina teaches us that life is too short – and sweet – to not dance to the beat of our own drum, whatever that may be.

'When I was a kid, I just wanted to sing on stage and, in that, I hoped to make people happy.'

How Sabrina Are You?

Picture this: it's 9pm, you've just had a long, hot bubble bath and you are now slipping into your favourite purple, sheer nightgown. You complete a deep-hydration facial cleanse, practise your gratitude and lock your phone away for the night. Soon you'll be catching those zzzs distraction-free. Does this routine sound familiar? Perhaps you're more like Sabrina Carpenter than you thought.

Intrigued to find out whether you have any other similarities with the pop princess herself? Take the 'how Sabrina are you?' quiz below ...

Side note: If you find you've got nothing in common with Sabrina, don't stress! Every human is unique and we're all perfect as we are. It would be boring if everyone was the same, don't you think?

What item do you always keep in your Dior tote? (OK, maybe not Dior, but we can dream!)

a. A mini essential oils kit
b. A hefty rose quartz crystal
c. A bag? What's that?

What's your cocktail of choice?

a. Limoncello spritz
b. Espresso martini
c. Piña colada

What's your favourite comfort food?

a. Chicken fajitas
b. Mac 'n' cheese
c. Pizza

Who would be your celebrity BFF?

a. Taylor Swift
b. Chappell Roan
c. Troye Sivan

If you could see anyone in concert, who would it be?

a. Christina Aguilera
b. ABBA
c. Rush

What is your go-to 'I just threw this on' look?

a. A babydoll dress and platform heels
b. A bubble skirt
c. Jeans and a nice top

Mostly As

Knock knock, who's there? It's Sabrina Carpenter's long-lost twin. When you're not boosting your mood with some essential oils, you're kicking back with your friends with a limoncello spritz or two ... or three. Basically, you couldn't be more like Sabrina if you tried. All that's left to do now is write another Grammy-winning album. Are you up for the challenge?

Mostly Bs

You've got loads in common with Sabrina, but you've also got your own thing going on. Whether that's practising crystal healing or thrifting for cute 60s' wardrobe staples, you and Sab would get on like a house on fire! It's giving best friends vibes.

Mostly Cs

Yeah, you might drive around with 'Espresso' on repeat, but that's as far as the similarities go. No worries, though, Sabrina's friendship group is very diverse and you'd 100 per cent make it into her inner circle. Like I said, it'd be no fun if everyone was the same. And you sound super fun anyway, so just roll with it, babes!

CHAPTER ONE

Era of the Pop Princess

bet u wanna be a star

Let's not forget that as an 11-year-old Sabrina was singing Adele into a hairbrush at home, and she was also gearing up for her first acting role. Enter the Sabrina small-screen era.

In 2011, the preteen got her first taste of the entertainment industry when she guest-starred in *Law & Order: Special Victims Unit*. She played a young girl named Paula, who was the victim of abuse, in a scene with Christopher Meloni's Detective Elliot Stabler. Though a small part, the role required maturity and sensitivity. Now, at 26 years old and worlds away from this tiny snippet of telly – both age-wise and professionally – many can see that it was a significant start to Sabrina's acting career.

Next up was Sabrina's first recurring role in the Fox sitcom *The Goodwin Games*. In the summer of 2012, she was cast as the young version of Chloe Goodwin and appeared in five episodes. The gig was a huge step up from *Law & Order*. She became a semi-regular character, and it was the first time Sabrina got to showcase her now-celebrated sense of humour. Many viewers expressed that they found Sabrina's performance hilarious and the delivery of her lines were funny and well-timed. That wise-cracking wit? She was born with it.

From these roles came more regular gigs, a sure-fire sign that Sabrina had officially got her foot in the industry door. Cue her first song with Disney and her debut professional musical offering. In 2013 her version of 'Smile', recorded for *Disney Fairies: Faith, Trust, and Pixie Dust,* was released. Inspired by the *Disney Fairies* film series, the track charted on Radio Disney. Then in 2013

'Not to be the person that brings up their astrology, but I'm a Taurus, and I think that might have something to do with the fact that I've always just been very driven. Some people like to call it stubborn. I like to say driven.'

Sabrina regularly voiced Princess Vivian in the animated fantasy children's television series, *Sofia the First*. Her supporting role as Sofia's friend, the music-loving princess of Zumaria, led to her performing the song 'All You Need' with Ariel Winter. The same year, she appeared in the dark, fantasy, comedy horror movie *Horns,* as the younger version of the main character, Merrin.

It comes as no surprise that Sabrina naturally found herself flourishing in the entertainment space from such a young age. Both of her parents, David and Elizabeth, hail from creative backgrounds; her mother is a former dancer, while her father was a member of a garage band with his friends.

In a 2018 interview with JJ Ryan, as part of his *Stars in Cars* series, Sabrina opened up about how she followed in her mum's dancing footsteps. She also revealed that Elizabeth took vocal lessons in the past, and in a sweet turn of events, Sabrina received training from the same coach when she was growing up.

As for her father, while Sabrina 'says he was in a band', she noted that David never pursued music professionally. Especially not to the chart-topping standards his daughter would one day reach. Despite her father's musical career being more of a casual affair, it's clear that there's a musical streak that runs through the Carpenter family.

Her three older sisters – Sarah, Shannon and Cayla – have also followed the family path into the arts; Sarah is a singer and photographer, Shannon is a dancer and Cayla is a hairstylist. What's more her aunt, Nancy Cartwright, is a well-known actress who, most notably, has voiced the iconic character of Bart Simpson on *The Simpsons* since 1987. For the millennials out there, Sabrina's aunty is also the voice behind Chuckie Finster in the Nickelodeon series *Rugrats*. Having family members passionate about the creative world – and finding success in their own lanes – undoubtedly contributed to Sabrina's ambitions and work ethic. From a young age she'd seen her closest allies embrace hard work. She had the mindset of, 'If I want something bad enough, I need to put in the effort.'

Sabrina has been very vocal about how much support she's received from them all, too. She told JJ Ryan that she'll 'always remember' how 'kind' and 'supportive' her family were while growing up, in nurturing her big dreams rather than shutting them down.

Granted, our heroine was lucky to have had such a strong support system around her, as humans are naturally social beings, and love and affection are fundamental needs. A familial support network can show itself in many ways, though, and whether it's blood-related or you choose your family of friends, it's important to have an inner circle. For our mental health, it's crucial we treasure the relationships that bless our lives with love and kindness.

In a 2019 interview with Urban Outfitters, Sabrina elaborated on this further and proved that her parents were not only willing to verbally support their daughter but act on it. When she was 10 years old, her father transformed a closet in the family home into a recording studio for the fledgling star. Painted entirely purple (because she was going through a 'purple phase' at school at the time), Sabrina recalled how her dad went to extreme lengths to make it as professional and fun as possible.

She remembers it as her first recording studio, and the first real place she had dedicated to recording her covers. In the same year as that interview she told *Marie Claire* that she 'really found comfort in the space,' despite being just a decade old.

To Disney-ing heights

You're probably wondering, what happened to Sabrina's acting career? Well, after her earlier smaller roles, Sabrina was clearly making a name for herself on the circuit. So something bigger, better and more career-enhancing was surely around the corner, right? Welcome to Sabrina Carpenter, the Disney star.

Take yourself back to 2014. Where were you? What were you doing? Sabrina was only 14 when she auditioned for a new show that had been commissioned by Disney. The series was called *Girl Meets World,* pitched as a new and updated version of the 90s coming-of-age sitcom.

Rather than following the original character Cory Matthews and his journey from elementary school to adulthood, this show would focus on a young girl called Riley Matthews. Fun fact: Sabrina actually auditioned for the lead role of Riley, but the casting team ultimately gave the opportunity to *Spy Kids* star Rowan Blanchard.

But that disappointment wasn't the end for a teenage Sabrina. Rumour has it that production was impressed with her performance but felt that she'd be better suited for the role of Maya Hart, Riley's best friend and sidekick. Apparently, Sabrina's naturally witty personality combined with her flair for dramatic acting were exactly what they had in mind for the character. This is because Maya's past was more complicated; her quick wit and wisdom beyond her years came from growing up in a single-parent household after being abandoned by her father.

As a friend, Maya is loyal, loving and the one who makes everybody laugh. This character trait came naturally to Sabrina, who has always been the biggest cheerleader for those closest to her. She often refers to her sisters as her 'best friends' and regularly mentions them, whether on social media or in interviews. She's revealed that the siblings share the same 'harsh sense of humour' and that no subject is off-limits. I don't know about you, but I'd love to be a fly on the wall at a Carpenter roasting session.

Acting credentials

Law & Order: Special Victims Unit: 2011

Orange Is the New Black: 2013

Horns: 2013

The Goodwin Games: 2013

Girl Meets World: 2014–2017

Adventures in Babysitting: 2016

The Hate U Give: 2018

The Short History of the Long Road: 2019

Tall Girl: 2019

Broadway's *Mean Girls*: 2020

Work It: 2020

Clouds: 2020

Emergency: 2022

Tall Girl 2: 2022

In Her Good Graces

Being in the spotlight from such a young age means Sabrina also has some pretty famous pals. One of her closest and longest friendships is with actress Joey King. But it's not exactly surprising that the two became buddies, considering they're both Disney kids. Meeting at a charity event 'many years ago', according to Sabrina, Joey has since echoed how close the pair are. One stalk of their Instagrams and you'll see for yourself. Their grids are littered with pictures together and gushing tributes to each other.

The sweetest nod to their friendship is perhaps Sabrina's post to Joey on her wedding day. Sharing a carousel of snaps from the event, she gushed over her 'wife' getting married and noted that she 'wept and wept'. Sabrina concluded the heartfelt message by saying how 'immensely lucky' she felt to have been a part of the couple's celebrations. Err, cute.

Sabrina has also developed a close bond with her inspiration, Taylor Swift. Their friendship dates back to 2021, when Tay sent Sabrina a *Red* care package. In the years since, Sabrina has declared Taylor to be one of her 'best, best friends'. Sabrina even coined the nickname 'taybrina' during the *Eras Tour*. If that's not friendship, I don't know what is.

'She's very supportive of me and knows who I am as a person.'

Self-care is essential

Whether you incorporate manifestation into your self-care routine or it's a military effort that requires scented candles, face masks and meditation afterwards, Sabrina knows the weight of wellness. She's previously shared the importance of finding a balance in her hectic life and taking the time to focus on herself. She's a busy woman, after all.

'Writing music has been my self-care. If I'm alone and I'm really stressed, I will be at my piano for hours on end.'

At its core, self-care is the intentional practice of engaging in activities that promote mental, emotional, physical and spiritual well-being. Whatever taking care of your own needs looks like – from adopting stress-management techniques, healthy habits or partaking in things that bring you joy – make sure you remember to put yourself first sometimes.

For Sabrina, it looks a little bit like this: staying present, enjoying the moment and commending herself for where she's at.

But what about the actions and activities she takes to maintain her self-care journey? Turns out, she's just like us. From indulging in an extra bubble bath – complete with salts, soaks and, dare I say it, a cheeky glass of wine – she also lives for a good walk. Fresh air is life, according to Sabrina.

'There's something about enjoying the little things that are really helpful for my mental health, whether just laughing with friends or doing things that feel outside of all of this.'

SABRINA'S TOP SELF-CARE TIPS

Firstly, bio-individuality is important to Sabrina. It's the concept that everyone is unique, and that embracing our individuality is the perfect recipe for health and happiness. During her 2022 *Marie Claire* interview, she said: 'Every time I've ever met someone that really was just so genuinely, authentically themselves, it's such a beautiful thing, and you can kind of feel that radiating off of them.'

So with that, what other self-care tips does Sabrina have?

- **Skincare:** For Sabrina, her skincare routine is the one time she gets to herself every day. It's incredibly important to her; it enhances her mood and sets her up for the day. Like a lot of us, she keeps it simple with the classic – but proven – cleanser, toner and sunscreen. 'Every time I do it, I automatically feel a lot better, and it makes me feel a little bit more centered,' Sabrina said.

- **Bedtime is a distraction-free zone:** That means no phones, computers or interferences from the outside world. To ensure good sleep hygiene, blue light exposure is a no-no. It suppresses melatonin, the hormone that regulates sleep and disrupts the body's sleep-wake cycle. Forget supplements and military sleep methods, all Sabrina needs to get her beauty sleep is a dark, quiet room. She said: 'I can't remember the last time I watched a TV show. By the end of the day, I feel like I've used up everything I have, so I just love sleep and getting to sleep as quickly as I can.'

- **Social media detox:** I can personally say that switching off from the online world is a lifesaver sometimes. And Sabrina's right: we don't realise how much we depend on social media and how much we consume it. The effects it can have on our mental health, especially if we're already in a low place, can be dangerous. Cue wise words from Sabrina that I couldn't have said better myself: 'We're consuming things we don't want to see, but it pops up in front of us, and it's there, and we're stuck with our feelings. But I think the best thing for me, sometimes, is to just not look at it.'

- **Make exercise a social event:** Often, the last thing we want to do after a long day at work or school is head to the gym. Usually, the thought of snuggling up on the sofa with your favourite reality show is a lot more appealing. Alas, no one is immune from having to exercise. But if you struggle with sticking to a workout routine, or you simply don't find it enjoyable, Sabrina recommends making it a social event. 'I love working out with friends because it makes me feel like I'm not working out.' Erm, convinced.

She's working late, 'cause she's a singer

Just before *Girl Meets World* debuted, the young actress released her first solo single. The song, 'Can't Blame a Girl for Trying' was everything you'd expect from a Disney teen: bubblegum pop, catchy lyrics and an overly smiley music video complete with Converse, roller skates and Sabrina casually strumming away on a tennis racket. The track was co-written by a young Meghan Trainor and released the same year that she burst onto the scene with 'All About That Bass'. What a year for pop!

Not long after, Sabrina's debut EP of the same title dropped, filled with similar songs about teenage crushes, navigating young adulthood, mistakes and moving on. But some of the themes – especially love and heartache – are still as prevalent in her music today as they were back then.

If a full-time job in a hit Disney show wasn't enough, Sabrina was now juggling her newfound fame as a music artist. A year into *Girl Meets World*, in 2015, she dropped her first full-length album, *Eyes Wide Open,* with Hollywood Records. The vibe of the record resonated with Sabrina's 'good girl next door' aesthetic and tackled obvious teenage topics of learning who you are, finding your path, friendship and love. Clean-cut and family-friendly, it was a classic Disney debut. Sabrina thought so, too. According to the star, the title song 'perfectly describe[d] a teenage girl'.

The song 'Eyes Wide Open' scooped a Radio Disney Music Award in the 'Best Anthem' category in 2016, and the album debuted at number 14 on the US *Billboard* Digital Albums charts.

As for Sabrina's musical style at the time, it followed in a similar vein to her EP, *Can't Blame a Girl for Trying*. The 12-track album was teen-pop and folk-pop-influenced, brimming with country, acoustic, pop rock and power pop. Songs like 'We'll Be the Stars' and, of course, the title track, offered listeners Sabrina's reflective side. Both explored the pressures of being young and famous, while simultaneously showing growth and maturity.

The album also marked the first time Sabrina dipped her toe into the songwriting pool, co-writing four songs. Years later, when 'Espresso' turned her into a global star, her producer, Julian Bunetta, described Sabrina as having a 'Rolodex of song ideas or titles in her head'. He told *Music Week* in 2024 that 'she likes to hear the song over and over so that everything is crystallised and it all has purpose.'

He also noted how he's learned so much from Sabrina. Mainly, to follow his gut instinct. 'Because if you don't absolutely love your song and would die for it, how do you expect anyone else to?' he mused.

However, before Sabrina reached said stratospheric heights, she'd go on to pen many songs in between. Her 2016 album, *EVOLution*, served to cement her as a serious songwriter and someone willing to work on her craft. (See? She's always had that grafters' attitude.) The album debuted at number

28 on the US *Billboard* 200. Sabrina penned nine out of 10 of the tracks.

During this era, she also opened for former Disney girl Ariana Grande during her 2017 *Dangerous Woman Tour*. Taking to the stage during the Brazil stops, Sabrina described the experience as 'insane' and 'beautiful'. She took the opportunity as a learning curve: watching Ariana perform left Sabrina in awe, while the 'accepting' crowd was everything she dreamed her own shows would one day be.

If you want proof that a 17-year-old Sabrina was quickly levelling up as a serious artist – and as a solid songwriter – look no further than the critics' opinions. The record was met with positive reviews, many crediting Sabrina's advancement since her debut. Like every Disney kid, who one daydreams of shaking off the Mickey Mouse shackles, Sabrina was on her way.

Christine M. Sellers of *The Celebrity Cafe* wrote: '[Sabrina] proves she's not just another Disney darling transitioning through her teenage years.' Rather, the album 'showcases Carpenter's growth as both a songwriter and a vocalist.'

Brittany Goldfield Rodrigues of *Andpop* said: 'With *EVOLution*, Sabrina is showing a mature musical side, willing to experiment with techno beats, lyrics and what she can do vocally. She provides an interesting indie yet synth take on pop music, and has clearly found a unique sound that she shines in, that separates her from the rest.'

Such comments must have been encouraging to hear. Knowing her work had substance, value and was appreciated not just by people her own age would have likely been the catalyst to hit the accelerator on her music career. Fast-forward to 2025, thank goodness she did.

EVOLution's maturity was surely part of the reason Sabrina took a big-girl step in the promotion circuit. In 2017, she landed a slot as the musical guest on *The Late Late Show with James Corden*. Back then, the *Gavin and Stacey* writer was dubbed the 'New King of Late Night TV'. He was also fresh from hosting the Grammys for the second time. Music and entertainment-wise, he was a pretty big deal. (Petition to revive *Carpool Karaoke* so the world can be blessed with a *Short n' Sweet* edition.)

Sabrina performed *EVOLution's* second single, 'Thumbs', which marked a shift from her previous teen-pop style. In fact, the whole album featured elements of dance-pop, R&B and electro-pop, while her music videos became less smiley and more sultry. Take the 'Thumbs' video. It's worlds away from the 'Eyes Wide Open' footage, which saw Sabrina looking pretty in a black tulle prom dress, singing her heart out in a grand hall. Instead, the video was gritty and slightly angry, taking place in a graffiti-stained train carriage. While still wearing all-black, Sabrina went for a twenty-first-century version of Sandy from *Grease's* 'You're the One That I Want' attire. Like the 1978 film, perhaps it was a metaphor for Sabrina's transition into adulthood. Just less of the flying cars.

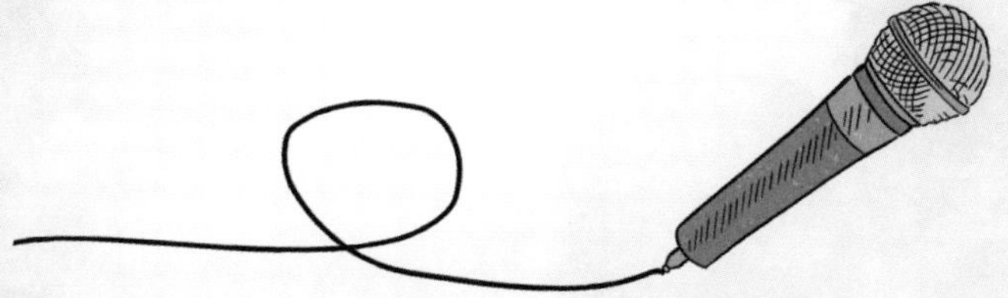

Perseverance and resilience

Unfortunately, not every talented person on this Earth will achieve their dreams of being a global popstar. That's just the way of the world. But, if you are – or once were – a small-town dreamer like Sabrina, it's nice to know that these dreams can come true.

However, alongside visualisation and belief, you also need to possess the two other keys to success: perseverance and resilience. Sabrina has both in spades, and her story is a testament to the power of both. She's faced challenges, setbacks and disappointments, but she's always bounced back up and powered through. 'Every time something hasn't worked out, it's always been because it led me to something that has worked out.'

Like any other human, there have also been times when Sabrina has found it hard to pick herself up and dust herself off. 'Sometimes I think to myself, "Wow, I made it through yesterday,"' she told *StyleCaster* in 2022. She admitted to continuously feeling that way. Sabrina added: 'I've been really shocked at my resilience and my perseverance. As things get harder and more confusing and trivialising, it's a really beautiful moment with yourself to know that you are capable of pushing through really tough times and always being able to find the light moments even in those really dark times.'

These are wise words, and ones that she would love to go back and tell her younger self if she had the chance. Though it's too late for that now, she can at least share this wisdom with us, her fans.

More cryptically, Sabrina has demonstrated resilience in her music. Arguably the most famous example is 'Feather', in which, through a campy pop beat, Sabrina sings about finding the strength to move on from a toxic relationship. More importantly, to learn, love, accept and respect yourself. Further hard evidence that the song oozes persistance comes from *Billboard,* who in a review wrote: '"Feather" is a powerful anthem about empowerment and resilience. It is a song that will stay with you long after you finish listening to it.'

On a side note: If you're prepared to put in the effort but also want to sprinkle some manifestation techniques into your work ethic for good measure, here are some top tips.

- **Identify your desires:** What is it you want and why? Be clear on your goals and define them with precision. Don't use vague language – if you can't be sure on what it is you want, the manifestation gods surely won't be able to either.

- **Write your goals down:** Putting your goals in writing makes them more tangible, and provides a place for you to focus your energy.

- **Visualisation:** Imagine your desires have come true. Try to picture yourself in vivid detail experiencing them – every sense needs to be activated. Think about how you'd feel having achieved your dreams; what emotions do you associate with it?

- **Affirmation:** It's no use journalling your desires just once. You need a dedicated book for your affirmations. Every morning and every night, write them down as many times as you feel necessary. Repeat them to yourself out loud – both your subconscious mind and the universe needs to hear and believe them, too.

- **Practise gratitude:** This is something Sabrina knows about only too well. Every morning, she makes a list of the things she's grateful for, which helps her to start her day on a positive note. This appreciation for what you already have helps to create a positive vibration, therefore attracting more positive vibes your way.

- **Release resistance:** Sabrina is also an expert here, too. Alongside her gratitude habit, she incorporates mindfulness into her daily routine. Release any resistance, negative thoughts or beliefs about yourself. Your manifestation needs a clear path.

- **From words, create action:** Chanting your affirmations to the moon every night simply won't do. You also need to be active with your goals. Whether little or big, try to take steps towards your desires. Moving forward is key.

- **Embrace the law of attraction:** This philosophy suggests that positive thoughts and beliefs attract positive experiences into your life. Likewise, negative thoughts and beliefs attract negative outcomes. Essentially, it's the idea that your thoughts and feelings have the power to shape your reality.

MANIFESTATION DON'TS:

- **Don't expect instant results:** Manifestation is a process that takes time. Don't be disheartened if after day one you're not a Grammy-winning popstar. Remember, you need to put in the effort. Then, when your dreams do finally come true, it'll feel all the more special, because you've earned it.

- **Clarity is key:** You can't manifest a vague goal.

- **Don't resist change:** Life is full of ups, downs, twists and turns. If everything goes exactly the way you planned, where's the fun in that? Embrace change and welcome new possibilities. Remember Sabrina's brief stint on Broadway? If she didn't embrace those changes, would she be the global pop phenomenon we know and love today?

‘Your gut is a very strong thing. The gut tells you a lot. And it might not tell you word for word what you’re thinking, but it gives you enough to know whether or not you feel good in an environment or not.’

The Disney Days are Over

Sabrina's good fortune at such a young age was not lost on her. Maya and her Disney family were her everyday existence for a huge portion of her life. Reflecting on the show, she told *Teen Vogue* in 2020: 'That was my world, and that was my everything, and I was so proud to be a part of it and all that it stood for.'

Sabrina also acknowledged that it kept her young and grounded. Disney stars are often caught in a loop of wanting to grow up, desperate to enter the next phase of their career, but afraid that if they stay cast in the butter-wouldn't-melt mould, they'll never escape it. The irony is, if the outside world let them mature naturally, without ostracising them for 'growing up too fast', the transition wouldn't be feared. In reality, they're just normal humans experiencing life in the spotlight. So, while 'mistakes' were made – which are expected from teenagers and need to take place in order for us to learn and find ourselves – Sabrina wouldn't change her Disney days for anything. 'I think the beauty of the show was that we really were at the age that we were playing, and we were coming into ourselves as we were playing characters that were coming into themselves,' she reminisced.

After a stint in a huge Disney show, there's always that one album that pushes a star over the edge from nearly adult to officially adult territory. So, in 2017, it felt almost fitting that *Girl Meets World* wrapped. Sabrina had already met the world, and the world had got to know – and love – her. Can we say she was entering her 'woman meets world' era? We'll save the global domination for later.

Sabrina's Slim Pickin's

***Juno* (2007) –** How could we not include this mid-noughties classic? Sabrina literally named her *Short n' Sweet* album track after it. As you might have guessed, it follows Juno, a 16-year-old highschooler who falls pregnant after sleeping with her friend and longtime admirer Paulie Bleeker. Convinced that she's not ready to be a mother, Juno makes a selfless decision for her unborn child, putting him up for adoption. The film stars alt icons Elliot Page and Michael Cera.

***Death Becomes Her* (1992) –** In this high-camp fantasy comedy, Helen and Madeline, two former friends-turned-rivals, consume a magic potion that promises eternal youth and beauty. When they 'perish' fighting over a man, they realise the elixir has rendered them 'undead.' Homework: Watch this film and then watch the 'Taste' video. I told you the similarities were uncanny!

***Alice in Wonderland* (2010)** – Of all the fairytale characters out there, Alice is the one who gives the biggest Sabrina Carpenter vibes. Whimsical, wide-eyed and wildly curious, like Sabrina, Alice has been identified as a cultural icon. As for the 2010 film, based on Lewis Carroll's Victorian novel *Alice's Adventures in Wonderland*, our heroine follows a rabbit in a blue coat to the magical wonderland from her dreams.

***Heathers* (1988) –** A little less wholesome, but a cult classic we can see Sabrina reworking in a remake, *Heathers* centres around Veronica, a high school student who is welcomed into the popular clique at her school. After clashing with the group's ruthless, bullying ways, Veronica and her new boyfriend, J.D, decide to kill off the cool kids one by one.

***Hook* (1991)** – Back to the fantasy world now, specifically Neverland. When Captain Hook abducts Peter Pan's kids in the *real* world, he has no choice but to return to the 'imaginary faraway place' to rescue them. There, he reunites with his old friends, the Lost Boys, and cheeky Tinkerbell, who is played to perfection by Julia Roberts.

***Kill Bill: Volume 1* (2003) –** Uma Thurman's 'The Bride' will forever be a cinematic icon. This Quentin Tarantino masterpiece is also another film Sabrina heavily referenced in her 'Taste' video. Hello? Jenna Ortega's nurse outfit and eye patch? It's Elle Driver 2.0. In terms of the plot, Thurman plays a pregnant assassin, code-named 'The Bride'. After being brutally attacked by her ex-boss, Bill – where she spent four years in a coma – she seeks revenge on him and his cronies. Her mission? Kill. Bill. And anyone else who gets in her way.

CHAPTER TWO

The ‘S’ in Sabrina stands for Star

Singularly Perfect

Sabrina's early version of saying, 'Look at me, I'm a grown-up now,' was the *Singular* period. In 2018, aged 19, she dropped *Singular: Act I*. She described the album as a coming-of-age story, one that reflects 'empowerment, confidence, and being comfortable with yourself regardless of what anybody thinks.'

It was a project she felt passionate about – not just because she was a credited songwriter on every track, but because the themes were different. Sabrina wasn't just singing about love and breakups, she was writing about moving on with total control over her life. Part of that autonomy shines through well in 'Sue Me'. In the cheekiest Sabrina way, of course.

For those unfamiliar with the context for this, in 2017 Sabrina was sued by two of her former music managers, Stan Rogow and Elliot Lurie, for breach of contract after they were fired in 2014. Although the case was eventually dismissed, it inspired a clapback album track disguised as a song about a romance. The confessional attitude and brashness of the lyrics have clearly stayed with Sabrina since then. Ain't no one making her cry, especially when she's done her makeup so nice.

Following *Act I's* release, revered indie music magazine *The Line of Best Fit* gushed that Sabrina had arrived as a 'fully-fledged star'. The review's title said it all, it read: 'Sabrina Carpenter has always displayed a knack for crafting – and curating – strong pop releases, but *Singular: Act I* sees her hone these skills further, resulting in her tightest, most polished project to date.'

This is just one example, but the release of the album opened up a whole new world of press coverage for Sabrina. In a 2018 interview with *W Magazine*, she revealed her excitement after seeing a 'huge bus' with her face on it. 'I was not prepared for that,' she said at the time. The reaction seems slightly humble from someone who'd been in the spotlight since the tender age of 11, don't you think?

It could be coincidence, it might not be, but these bigger feats may have helped Sabrina find her voice in the studio. In the past, she likely let producers, writers and engineers guide her through sessions. Understandably, too. She was young, inexperienced and still learning the tricks of the trade as she went. The album names could also have been a literal sign that she was ready to take the reins. Sabrina continued: 'There were times when I was 15 or 16 and I'd be in the recording studio singing and do some vibrato, and people would be like, "Can you just keep it straight?" Then I realised later, wait, that's my voice. You don't realise until later that those little things make me Sabrina and differentiate me from different people.'

In hindsight, it's nice to know that she was recognising her uniqueness, and wanted to let it shine. These quirks of ours – in whatever talent or hobby they reveal themselves – are what make us special. If it's not hurting anybody, why change for other people?

And if you needed any more evidence that she was growing up, how about this for a monologue:

'The concept that I found for this album later on was that I wasn't writing about confidence; I could just hear a new confidence embodied throughout it.'

'I know myself better than anybody, and I know my fans better than anybody, and that was one thing I had to constantly fight to get people to pay attention to. If you tell an artist how to be an artist, then they aren't going to be an artist. That is such a sound bite, but it's true. I had to start taking control and really capitalise on that confidence.'

During this time, Sabrina's musical maturity was parallel with her acting career. Just one month before the release of *Singular: Act I*, she starred in the coming-of-age teen drama *The Hate U Give.* The film follows a young Black girl named Starr who witnesses the fatal shooting of her childhood friend, Khalil, at the hands of a police officer. Facing pressure from various communities, she must fight for what's right. Sabrina played Hailey Grant, one of Starr's school friends. She described the character as a 'mean girl', 'ignorant' and a step away from the 'likeable' roles she'd been known for. After its release the movie received rave reviews for how it handled the Black Lives Matter topic within a young adult film space.

Sabrina elaborated: 'It was exactly what I had hoped we would start to see in this younger demographic. I think that for a long time people felt like you had to dumb it down. At 10 years old people always said, "You're so mature for your age", and I wish there were things like this when I was young, and things to describe the way that the world was working at that time.'

We must not forget that from an early age Sabrina found herself surrounded by people much older than her, due to her career. Such a profound comment is the product of the unique experiences *she* had growing up, juggling being a young girl and a professional entertainer – which forced her to be conscious of the messages she shared with her fans.

Too often, the complexity of life during the tween and teen years is not taken seriously, and as a group, they're underestimated. Sabrina proves this is not always the case: she's very respectful, which helps to paint her generation in a positive light, too.

Sabrina inevitably received backlash for *Singular*. When talking to *Billboard* in 2018, she explained how, for a long time, people knew her as a fictional TV character. A character who had lines written for her and an attitude created for her. It was not the real Sabrina. So when she started releasing music, people subconsciously assumed it was still all an act.

Sabrina expanded: 'For a lot of people, their first impression of me was as a 13-year-old girl [singing] the kinds of songs that she should be singing. Then, flash-forward to 19, and people are asking why I am not singing about the same things that I did when I was 13, as if that's normal.'

She's not wrong. If she'd released the album as a brand-new artist, nobody would have questioned anything. But because of her history, she knew the comparisons and resistance would one day come. 'It's always something that I'll have to deal with and get over. Not in a bad way –

in a way that I hope they can digest it and come to like it, like I have,' Sabrina concluded.

Eight months after *Singular*: *Act I* showed the world she meant business, *Act II* demonstrated Sabrina's more vulnerable side. She told *Marie Claire* in 2019 that it was her most 'personal album yet'. The first track, 'In My Bed', immediately proved she wasn't lying. Despite kicking the record off with a synth-soaked, electro-kissed atmosphere, Sabrina explained that her lyricism was a lot darker. Taking on themes of anxiety and feeling overwhelmed, and showcasing lower moments where 'life feels like a lot to deal with', she described it to *People* as 'opening the door' to *Act II.*

'The song is about one of those moments where life feels like a lot to deal with. We took that and turned it into something really fun and vulnerable.'

Quite aptly, the lead single from *Act II* was 'Pushing 20'. No better way to celebrate leaving your teenage years, hey? The song drew comparisons to Rihanna's *ANTI* era, thanks to the trap and hip-hop influence.

As for the themes, the coming-of-age element feels perfect. Sabrina revealed the 'organic' process of the writing session and that the track highlights living in the moment, not overthinking things and dealing with your own responsibilities rather than worrying about what everyone else thinks. That's the great thing about growing up. You learn to love, respect and trust yourself more. Your confidence in yourself grows and it becomes visible from the inside out.

Critics approved, too. *Paper* magazine's Brendan Wetmore dubbed the whole album as a 'culmination of pop eras – a rich plurality that separates itself from anything modern hit-writing has tried to glue together in recent years.' That, and how the album is 'truly a great standalone pop record.'

For those who purchased the album, you'll remember Sabrina's personal note tucked away in the booklet. Looking back now, it almost feels like an admission that she was ready to level up. It also felt like a farewell to this section of her music career, as the album was her last with Hollywood Records.

The message read: 'For this second act and closing chapter of the show I ask you to listen intently, and remember in life, there are 2 sides to every story. This is my side. With each number, I hope you find your own stories within them.'

Fate had different plans

Every single person on this planet dealt with COVID differently. For the introverts (who were lucky, healthy and privileged enough not to have been physically affected by the virus), it was a welcome break to check out of reality and check in with oneself. For those questioning their futures (and who were granted temporary paid lay-offs from work), it was a chance to figure out what one truly wanted and spend the time in limbo working towards that goal. For people like Sabrina, who seemed to have everything and were only going up, it was a bit of an odd one.

In March 2020, she landed her Broadway debut, being cast as Cady Heron in the stage version of *Mean Girls*. She was 'thrilled' and 'excited' for the opportunity – who wouldn't be? Broadway is a *big* deal. However, after three months of non-stop rehearsals and two performances, the show abruptly ended as the world came to a complete standstill. For the next year, Sabrina had no idea when she'd next take to the stage. It wasn't until January 2021 that the musical officially announced its closure due to the ongoing health crisis.

Who knows? If planet Earth hadn't turned upside-down the Grammy-winning Sabrina we know today may never have come to fruition. She might have followed the Broadway path, never to have gone viral for concocting a cheeky outro for 'Nonsense'.

A journal a day keeps the heartache at bay

Have you ever tried ... journalling? Before you go to bed tonight, grab a notebook and write down everything that happened today, along with how it made you feel. Even the mundane stuff, like doing the laundry or going to the shops to get milk. Tomorrow, do the same thing again. And again. And again. Until one day, you have pages of your own life story, reminders of your past and hopes for your future.

While Sabrina's version of journalling is through song, sharing snippets of her life with the world, both have the same effect. It's a safe space to explore your feelings, ask questions, set goals and enhance mental clarity. Unsure where to start? Use these prompts to get you going:

How am I feeling today?
What are my top priorities for today? What did I learn?

What am I grateful for right now?
What are three things I'm grateful for today?

What negative emotions and energies am I holding on to?
Why do I feel this way?

What am I looking forward to this week?
What steps can I take to get closer to my goal?

'It's taking that second to remind yourself that just because you have so much to be grateful for doesn't mean that there aren't things you're internally struggling with.'

She Had to Jump the Octave

Alas, while the pre-*Short n' Sweet* days paved the way for stadium-worthy Sabrina, the move to a more grown-up label would eventually leave her feeling distanced from her old discography.

In 2021, Sabrina signed a deal with Island Records. Not only did this switch pay off (as we all know), but it helped her officially make *the* move. As soon as she signed on that dotted line she was no longer a part of the Disney franchise. It was in writing. The tulle négligés, suspenders and bejewelled platform boots were calling.

On signing with Island, she told *Variety* that it was the 'perfect place for [her] to start the next chapter of [her] music career and evolution as an artist.' Don't get her wrong, she was immensely proud of her catalogue and grateful for where it took her. It's just that entering a new decade saw her looking forward, not backwards.

'For the people who love those early records and listen to them, I love you for that. But I personally feel a sense of separation from them, largely due to the shift in who I am as a person and as an artist, pre-pandemic and post-pandemic.'

So, Carpenters, phones at the ready, because we're about to *not* send some emails, if you get my drift. In July 2022, Sabrina dropped her first album with Island, and boy, we were not ready. *Emails I Can't Send* was undoubtedly her most confessional piece of work yet. It was also one of the hardest for her to write, let alone release to the world to be judged. Thankfully, she did, because it debuted at No. 23 on the *Billboard* 200. At the time, it was her highest chart entry to date.

Complete with an intensity only possible through strained familial relations and infidelity, Sabrina told *V Magazine* in 2023: 'A lot of it came from a really painful point in my life. It was a challenge to push myself throughout the process.' Fans have since praised the singer's transparency, in return, chanting her lyrics back to her on stage. 'There were moments I felt so isolated, and those are the moments people pick out and scream at the top of their lungs on tour.'

In a stroke of genius, or maybe even frustration, the album is made up of emails she literally couldn't send. Sabrina admitted to *Teen Vogue* that many of the song lyrics were plucked from emails she wrote to herself during the pandemic. Either slipping them straight into the tracks or developing the feelings into a more pop-friendly shape, it served as a form of therapy as she navigated her heartbreak.

At one point during the album-making process, things got a little too much for Sabrina. If you listen closely, you'll hear that many of the final takes on the record are demo vocals. Every creative person will tell you that while making art is a personal experience, it can take you to some of your lowest depths. But such lows can become the catalyst for some of your best work.

'Someone I looked up to let me down and it changed the way I love and receive love.'

Emotions aside, can we all take a minute to appreciate Sabrina's next achievement? By now, we all know that she's proved herself as a prolific songwriter, penning most of her albums to date alongside other writers. But due to the personal nature of *Emails I Can't Send,* it made sense for Sabrina to go entirely solo during some points in the album. For two tracks, 'emails i can't send' and 'how many things', Sabrina is the only writer credited. We love to see an artist coming out of their shell and growing in confidence!

When looking at the writers on the track listing, four familiar names pop up: Steph Jones, Amy Allen, Julia Michaels and John Ryan. Between the four of them, they boast Grammy Awards and nominations for prestigious titles, including the MTV Video Music Awards, *Billboard* Music Awards and the American Music Awards. Collectively, they've worked with everyone from Harry Styles, Britney Spears, Selena Gomez, Olivia Rodrigo, JADE, Florence + the Machine, Leon Bridges and Justin Bieber, to name a few. Check out the credited songwriters on *Short n' Sweet*, and you'll find them littered throughout the Grammy-winning album.

At the time of *Emails I Can't Send,* Steph, Amy, Julia and John were prolific, established writers. Partnering with them was a smart move for Sabrina *and* Island Records.

'I've really honed in on the people that I love making music with.'

As if by magic, Sabrina's first single on Island (before *Emails I Can't Send* dropped) was 'Skin' in 2021. Co-written with Ryan McMahon, another writer famed for working with artists such as Bebe Rexha, Tove Lo and Marina (and the recipient of a *Billboard* Music Award), the track was Sabrina's first *Billboard* Hot 100 entry. It peaked at number 48.

Legend has it, 'Skin' was Sabrina's response track to 'drivers license', the song that ironically catapulted Olivia Rodrigo from fellow Disney darling to pop princess. For the chronically online amongst us, you'll know both songs are rumoured to be about the love triangle between Sabrina and Olivia and her *High School Musical: The Musical* cast mate Joshua Bassett.

Olivia and Joshua reportedly dated from 2019 to 2020, while Sabrina and Joshua were thought to have been an item in

2021. Even though the romance made major headlines in their fan circles, Sabrina and Joshua have never actually confirmed their relationship. Funnily enough, many believe *Emails I Can't Send*'s 'because i liked a boy' is also about the sticky situation. To stir the pot even more, Joshua's 2021 track, 'Lie Lie Lie' was allegedly penned about the whole awkward fiasco. So, while the Oliva–Joshua–Sabrina entanglement may be written in Gen-Z drama history (and probably best left there), at least we got a couple of pop bangers from it.

Whether thanks to the above or not, *Emails I Can't Send* came during a time of intense attention into Sabrina's personal life. Having such an intimate album allowed her to reclaim her narrative and push her side of the story into the spotlight. The last song on the album, 'decode', holds a soft spot in Sabrina's heart. It explores both learning to accept and struggling to accept – weaving between blaming yourself for a situation and understanding there's nothing you can do to change things.

She delved deeper into the meaning of the track with *Glamour* in 2023, explaining why she feels such a strong connection with it. 'I'll always be going back to that theme. I think I'll always need to remind myself, "You can make it to the other end of things and just accept things as they are and let it be." And that song is really acceptance 101, which is a thing that we need to remind ourselves of constantly. We don't just learn it once, and then we're good. I'll be coming back for probably a long time.'

because i liked a boy

Sabrina's musical catalogue is a hybrid of relationship complexities, infatuation, heartbreak and the dynamics of love and dating. While 'Taste' and 'because i liked a boy' are rumoured to be about love triangles and past relationships, 'Feather' explores the freedom of moving on and letting go.

As for *Short n' Sweet*, and how Sabrina landed on the title, she told Zane Lowe in 2024 that it's related to so much more than just her physical appearance. As the record is littered with songs about relationships, Sabrina explained that she handpicked them based on two reasons. One was that some of the relationships were the shortest she ever had but affected her the most. Secondly, when responding to situations – be it in love or life in general – Sabrina was very honest about the fact that sometimes she reacts in a 'very nice' manner, while other times, 'it's not very nice'. The deeper meaning in this is that no one is perfect. But as long as you own your mistakes, strive to be the best version of you, and open yourself up to feel as deeply as possible, you're on the right path.

'I've always yearned to care enough about a person or a situation or a relationship in my life that it provokes that much feeling in me. Because I think that's why we're here,' she added.

As for advice on love and relationships, whether it's from *Short n' Sweet* or the earlier days, here's what we can learn from Sabrina, track by track:

'Almost Love' – In *Singular: Act I,* Sabrina explores life beyond casual dating. She exposes herself to the potential heartbreak of entering into a deeper, more meaningful relationship. To be vulnerable is to commit to another person without knowing the outcome. Sabrina told *Teen Vogue:* '"Almost Love" for me is kind of my life story. It's these vignettes of relationships that never have the ending that you imagine or the perfect ending, which I think is not realistic.'

'Good Graces' – In older Sabrina we meet a more confident, self-assured woman. She's setting boundaries and telling her partner that, yes, she will love and be there for you, but if you don't treat her well, she is not afraid to walk away. Here, Sabrina shows strength, maturity and the importance of knowing your self-worth.

'Lie to Girls' – Even though you're older and wiser, no one is exempt from the crazy things that being in love can make you do. Sabrina's *Short n' Sweet* era flits between the above and knowingly deceiving yourself. Sabrina says we can all be victims of overlooking someone's red flags because we're in love. We want this relationship to work, and we love the idea of it, but that's the problem – the idea is not real life.

'Don't Smile' – We've all been there: in the midst of a breakup and wanting our ex to be just as heartbroken as we are. Unfortunately, that's not always reality either. In this situation, time is a healer. Never forget your worth. Sometimes, relationships just don't work out, and that's OK.

'Please Please Please' – Here Sabrina sings about being infatuated with someone who keeps letting her down. Though presented from a 'bad boy' angle, with the protagonist worried that their partner's reputation will destroy their relationship and their pride, at the crux of it she's pleading for someone's attention and love. It's an example of how people will put up with anything – even if it's not right – for the sake of love. We all need and crave it, after all.

Sabrina-lit class over, it's time to close the chapter with some solid relationship wisdom from the woman herself. Back in 2023, Sabrina teamed up with Capital Radio to answer fan emails and offer them advice, especially when it comes to love. A fitting promo exercise for the *Emails I Can't Send* era, it also proved Sabrina's worth as a quality agony aunt. Hey, if she hadn't taken the musician road, maybe Sabrina could have lived a successful life with her own column ...?

ADVICE ON GETTING OVER HEARTBREAK

One fan opened their email by complimenting the album's title track. They said it 'really resonated' with them after they were cheated on. 'Now I have trust issues about whether I can ever fall in love again,' the fan admitted, then asked: 'How do I get out of this rut and get back on some dating apps?'

Enter Sabrina's on-the-nose response: 'That's a really awful place to be, and it makes you question a lot about yourself, when in reality it has nothing to do with you.' On how to get 'out of the rut' she said: 'I think you sort of just have to put it into perspective of, one: don't rush yourself, wait til you're ready, and whatever is meant for you will find you ... effortlessly.'

DATING GREEN FLAGS

From red to green, one fan asked what Sabrina classes as positive qualities in a partner. Her reply, 'We love when they're super communicative and consistent.' Tick, tick and tick.

And finally, a dilemma we've all experienced. Though not necessarily romantic, the feelings of abandonment are real. One fan asked: 'Hey Sabrina, I have the same barber week after week. He's a really nice guy. Last time I went in there, though, he wasn't available so I went to the other barber in the shop. He cut my hair so much better. Am I cheating on my barber if I stick with the new guy? Like, is this a breakup?' Sabrina teased: 'I think part of life is growing and changing. Just be honest. It's not cheating, and it's not a breakup. It's just a haircut. Hope it looks good. Love, Sabs.'

NONSENSE

Sabrina Carpenter is really famous
Some say she empowers, others 'tasteless'
Me? I think that she's a big ol' genius

Need a hint as to what track we're jumping into next? After the 2022 leg of Sabrina's *Emails I Can't Send Tour* sold out in less than a day, fans were concerned about one thing only: what NSFW outro would she ad-lib to 'Nonsense'?

The track was already a viral sensation on TikTok, with content creators using the sped-up version on the platform. People were dueting with the track or simply using it as background music to accompany their videos. Whatever they were doing, fan engagement was *high.* On 8 December 2022, Sabrina premiered the 'Nonsense' filter, which catapulted the song – and her fame – to further heights. In the hours after posting, 'Nonsense' experienced its biggest day-to-day streaming increase since it was released.

So, the only next sensible thing to do were the outros. It was customary for fans to check out the ad-libs from previous shows for clues about the next one. Often, all you had to do was figure out what innuendo rhymed with the city. Sabrina rhyming chakras with Osaka will never not be legendary.

They always say good things happen when you least expect it. So the fact that Sabrina never intended to write 'Nonsense' kind of explains its success. She was actually trying to write a ballad but was suffering from writer's block. According to Sabrina, she didn't even know what was going through her head when she wrote it – other than the fact that she might have been hungry. (Peak Sabrina humour if ever I've heard it.) She told Hits Radio in 2023 that her favourite part of writing is that 'you start the day without them and then you end the day with a song. It's special.'

She added: 'It was kind of redirection by fate. I was writing another song which was quite sad and slow, I couldn't really finish it. Maybe probably because I wasn't really in the headspace.' As for 'Nonsense', Sabrina continued: 'There's a lot of humour infused in the song, which is very similar to how I feel when I'm kind of crushing on somebody the first time. Maybe it's a little too close to home!'

Whether or not this mystery person knew Sabrina was falling hard, her fans had fallen harder. She couldn't comprehend their relationship with the song, finding it impossible to accept the concept of having penned a viral hit. During the interview with Hits Radio, her modest roots shone through: 'I feel like it's cool when people are like "oh I love your song!", "I know your song!"' she said. 'But I don't know, it takes like hammering it in, which I just try to stay away and let people enjoy it. It's been really cool to see the reaction on tour, I think that's probably like the first time that I realised that it was a fan favourite.'

From *Emails I Can't Send* came the deluxe edition: *Emails I Can't Send Fwd* in 2023. Yes, clever. The new songs continued with the pop/folk-pop/electropop/dance-pop genres and were announced through an Instagram post crafted in an email format. This was *not* a drill, guys. Sabrina really was blessing the soundscape with four more pop bobs: 'opposite', 'Feather', 'Lonesome' and 'things i wish you said'.

In her Insta caption, she addressed herself as 'email girl', and expressed her gratitude for the album's success. She said: 'For those of you that found a little piece of yourselves in this album, think of these few new songs as my sincerest thank you to you.' Sabrina added how 'so much happened in this chapter of [her] life,' that the songs kept pouring out of her. 'Ultimately, I couldn't stop writing, and still can't,' she mused. 'Email girl' then signed off, sharing that the new songs belong to the fans who were 'kind enough to make this record feel so welcome and heard.'

There's no denying: *Emails I Can't Send 2.0* was heard loud and clear. Come on – apart from Sinéad O'Connor or Madonna – what artist can say they've sparked outrage from the Catholic Church? Granted, Sabrina didn't stage a protest on *Saturday Night Live*. She did, however, dance provocatively in a black tulle mini dress and veil in front of the Blessed Virgin Mary Church's altar.

This video offended the Roman Catholic Diocese of Brooklyn so much that the church's pastor, Monsignor Jamie Gigantiello, was stripped of his administrative duties. Sabrina even addressed her thoughts on the matter during her 2024 Coachella performance. In classic Sabrina humour, she took to the stage wearing a 'Jesus Was a Carpenter' T-shirt. In hindsight, isn't it funny how 'Feather', a light-hearted post-breakup track that celebrates freedom caused such chaos? I'm calling it the 'Sabrina Effect'.

Though maybe not the church so much nowadays, Sabrina's dance routines and 'risqué' tour outfits are still causing some controversy – especially amongst the 'mum community'. (We're looking at you, Eiffel Tower.) Ever since the 'glow up' from Disney kid to her flirtatious version of Jessica Rabbit, Sabrina has admitted that some parents have problems with the content of her shows. 'You still get the occasional mother that has a strong opinion on how you should be dressing. And to that I just say, don't come to the show, and that's OK,' she told Capital in 2024.

The sad thing is, Sabrina wishes that people would take a minute to assess the global scale of her predicament. In her 2024 *Time Magazine* interview, she called it 'unfortunate' that her character is something that has had to be criticised. She said: 'Because truthfully, the scariest thing in the world is getting up on a stage in front of that many people and having to perform as if it's nothing. If the one thing that helps you do that is the way you feel comfortable dressing, then that's what you've got to do.'

'Femininity is something that I've always embraced. And if right now that means corsets and garter belts and fuzzy robes or whatever, then that's what that means.'

Embracing authenticity and growth

'When I was a kid, I just wanted to sing on stage and, in that, I hoped to make people happy,' Sabrina told *The Guardian* in 2024. When it all boils down to it, nothing much has changed; for that's exactly what she's done. So let's start there, shall we?

Musically, Sabrina has allowed herself to evolve authentically. She told *Billboard* in 2020 that her goal has always been to make music that reflects who she is as a person. Which means if something changes in her career or personal life, if she forges new relationships – romantic or platonic – or she simply grows up, her music should be allowed to transition with her.

'I think it's important to grow and change as an artist.'

Not to overuse the word authentic, but Sabrina has never wavered from this stance. My point's proven already, right? But humour me for a sec: remember when she said she felt a disconnect to her pre-*Emails I Can't Send* days, and that she wouldn't be performing them anymore due to embracing more personal and honest storytelling? Or when she stated that *Short n' Sweet* was her sophomore album, despite it actually being her sixth? Or how about the times she's openly said that she doesn't see a problem with switching genres – if she likes something and it works, she'll write it. *That's* the definition of authenticity. Essentially, Sabrina not confining herself to one style of music and only releasing records she can identify with demonstrates her growth as an artist.

Being so headstrong makes her stand out for another reason: the commercial music industry is renowned for demanding conformity. As much as I hate to say it, at the end of the day it's all about money. Labels look at the figures to see what sells, then they often try to replicate that with other artists. However, Sabrina has always rejected this cycle. Like a true artist, you don't go into this business for money; you do it for the love of your creations. But, having such a strong drive and belief inside of you eventually forces others to listen and watch. Even if you don't feel it inside, confidence demands authority. Follow your heart, and success will come.

In the decades when Sabrina has been on the scene, such confidence has definitely paid off. Especially when it comes to fellow faces in the industry. Singer and actress Hailee Steinfeld has known Sabrina for years, thanks to the pair working and walking in the same circles. In a 2021 interview with *Teen Vogue,* Hailee said: 'Sabrina is fearless in her approach to music and life. She's not afraid to show her authentic self, and that's incredibly inspiring.'

From distinct music to a distinct aesthetic, if someone showed you a picture of Sabrina's silhouette you'd instantly know it was her. These days, her look is very much flirty, fun and feminine, blending retro and modern elements to create her unique character.

Taybrina: the pop duo you always knew you needed

What's the next natural step after your own sold-out tour? You join the biggest and most celebrated world tour to ever exist, of course.

By now, there was no stopping Sabrina. From fans to critics to grandmas, everyone knew her name and everyone knew she was a big deal. 'Pop's next big thing' was a title she'd worn and worn out. She was firmly seated in the 'best in pop' category.

Taylor Swift confirmed this, personally asking Sabrina to join the *Eras Tour*. Being a major Swiftie, I honestly don't know how I'd react if I was approached in this way by one of my heroes. Probably the same as Sabrina, to be honest: 'I'm not gonna say I peed my pants because that sounds really graphic and maybe not sanitary, but I think it really just caught me off guard,' she told *Who What Wear,* adding that it was 'very much a childhood dream come true'.

And so, in the summer of 2023, off Sabrina skipped to Latin America, Australia and Singapore as the official opening act. Taylor later called Sabrina the 'pop princess of [her] dreams'.

Joining the *Eras Tour* was a long time coming, too. In 2010, Sabrina emotionally tweeted how 'amazing' the Taylor Swift concert was and cutely manifested how she 'can't wait to have a world tour someday like hers' with 'two sold-out shows'. May we direct you to her *Short n' Sweet Tour,* which kicked off in September 2024 and promptly sold out.

Or how about her childhood defeat in 2009, when she mourned not being able to enter a Taylor Swift karaoke contest to 'win tickets and a chance to meet her' because she wasn't 13? In 2024, the official *Eras Tour* X account spotlighted this moment, writing: 'Sabrina Carpenter really went from not being able to enter a karaoke contest to meet Taylor Swift in 2009 to performing with her live 15 years later.'

In March 2024 the *Eras Tour* wrapped up. It was an emotional time for Sabrina, almost bittersweet. How would it be possible to top the last seven months, travelling the world, living your biggest dream?

To mark the monumental moment, Sabrina posted a carousel of her 'best bits' from the tour. Snaps included black-and-white shots on stage, panoramic views of the adoring crowd, backstage antics and a photo of the new besties – Tay and Sabrina – during that viral trip to Australia Zoo.

You can tell the caption was from the heart; Sabrina taking a step back to ask herself, 'Did that really just happen?' She penned: 'That's a wrap for us on the eras tour: sitting at home reflecting on what a whirlwind this was and how very honoured I feel to have been part of it. I want to thank every crowd for being so welcoming and generous to us and making some of the most impressive friendship bracelets I've ever received, also a huge thank you to the incredible crew for being so hardworking and talented.'

And finally? 'The most thank yous I've ever thank you'd to Taylor,' Sabrina continued, adding how lucky she felt to have witnessed the 'magic' that is Taylor Swift and her tour. 'There is truly no one like you and there never will be! i love you with all my heart and i will cherish this taybrina era (and all the eras) till the end of time.'

Like Taylor, Sabrina's brand is a marketer's dream. Whenever she has a show, companies get creative with their marketing efforts. Take one of the *Short n' Sweet* concerts at the O2 Arena in London. The Pret A Manger in the local station took the initiative to advertise a 'Short Espresso' and a 'Sweet Raspberry Lemonade Cooler' promoted in Sabrina's cursive font. The cafe chain also plastered a huge love heart across the window, complete with pink glitter curtains to tempt fans inside for a pre-show drink. On the Tube, haircare brand Redken 5th Avenue N.Y.C. showcased their collaboration with Sabrina on the escalators. They even had a pop-up hair station inside the O2, offering product samples, styling services and a Sabrina photobooth experience prior to the show.

Everywhere you looked, you saw Sabrina's face. Commitment like this is rare. Businesses wouldn't do it if it didn't pay off.

If it's even possible, maybe Sabrina's popularity will skyrocket further, allowing her to command her own version of the *Eras Tour* one day. In the nicest way, she's already coming for Taylor: in March 2025 Sabrina scored another number one on *Billboard*'s Pop Airplay chart with 'Bed Chem'. The track followed in the footsteps of earlier hits including 'Taste', 'Please Please Please' and 'Espresso'. This meant *Short n' Sweet* became the first album to have four Pop Airplay number ones since Taylor Swift's *1989* back in 2014–15.

But back to 2024, and with a huge career bucket list ticked off, Sabrina couldn't sit and reflect for long. Following her last *Eras Tour* performance in Singapore, she hinted that *her* new era was coming. Sabrina told *Cosmopolitan:* 'I'm starting to feel like I've outgrown the songs I'm singing, which is always an exciting feeling because I think that means the next chapter is around the corner.'

Hello, 'Espresso'.

Espresso martini

Again, it would be rude – and foolish – not to. Don't worry, this cocktail can be made sans alcohol and sans caffeine, so everyone can enjoy it!

Instant espresso
Non-alcoholic vodka
Non-alcoholic coffee spirit
Vanilla extract
Maple syrup
Canned coconut cream
Coffee beans, to garnish

1. Prepare a serving of instant espresso mixed with boiling-hot water to dissolve.
2. Combine all the ingredients in a cocktail shaker and shake vigorously.
3. Finally, strain and serve the mix into a coupe cocktail glass (extra points if you've got Sabrina's version) and garnish with three coffee beans.

Fancy an Espresso?

The song dropped the day before Sabrina's debut Coachella performance and was instantly a viral hit across the globe. Outside of the US, 'Espresso' topped the charts in over 20 countries, including the UK, Australia, Ireland, Belgium and Norway. It also became Sabrina's first top 10 hit on the *Billboard* Global 200 chart and her first ever UK Number 1 single. In a niche turn of events, the Official Charts confirmed that 'Espresso' was the highest-charting song about caffeine in 24 years, since All Saints' 2000 hit 'Black Coffee'.

Critics described it as an 'instant earworm', from the witty, whimsical (and famously grammatically incorrect) lyrics to the pop, funk and dance elements. Sabrina's playful spirit also shone bright, with 'Espresso' being a metaphor for the intense, sometimes addictive effect that another person can have on you. Sabrina had this effect on her fans, too. The song was one of the hits – if not *the* hit – of summer 2024. Whether on holiday around the pool, at the bar with your pals or working Spotify's algorithm, 'Espresso' was *everywhere.*

Ariana Grande's 2024 *Saturday Night Live* 'Domingo' sketch proved that 'Espresso' had taken on a life of its own. Ariana parodied the song as part of a bridesmaid troupe, where the four friends outed the bride Kelsey for cheating on her new husband, Matthew, with a mystery man named Domingo. Ariana and co sang purposefully off pitch, prompting Sabrina to respond on Instagram with the sarcastic: 'Very nice and on pitch.' The sketch blew up on TikTok, garnering 102 million views on the platform. As part of the sketches for the *SNL50* anniversary special in February 2025, Sabrina joined the line-up for *Domingo: Vow Renewal.* Again parodying 'Espresso', Sabrina and the fellow bridesmaids recalled another girls' trip where, you guessed it, Kelsey hooked up with Domingo. Very silly, very funny, very stupid. But proof that the song had made it into the cultural zeitgeist.

Meanwhile, while it is unlikely that Sabrina was thinking about food-brand deals when she wrote 'Espresso', with such a huge hit on her hands that just so happened to be named after a popular beverage, it would have been foolish not to profit from it.

In November 2024 (and just in time for Christmas), it was reported that Sabrina had teamed up with Absolut Vodka and Kahlúa to release her own 'Short n' Sweet Espresso Martini Kit'. Complete with all the ingredients to make your own espresso martini, a coupe glass embellished with a festive ribbon and an edible cocktail topper in the shape of Sabrina's signature kiss mark, it was a glaringly obvious gimmick and perfect marketing for Absolut and the Carpenter brand. One month later, she collaborated with Dunkin' Donuts, releasing 'Sabrina's Brown Sugar Shakin' Espresso'. At this point, we should have permission to change the lyrics to, 'She's working late, cos she's Kris Jenner.'

Finding strength in vulnerability

In a constantly online world, it can be a scary thing to expose your deepest emotions. The minute you press send, there's no going back. You've let people in, and whether you like it or not, some people will be out there ready to judge.

While the majority out there embrace Sabrina with open arms, readily available to pick up her up when she's feeling down, for some reason it's the trolls who penetrate through the positives. Sabrina has previously opened up about receiving online hate. Although she knows it comes with the territory – and, sadly, is inevitable – she's still human, and it can hurt.

In 2023, she delved into this subject with *Glamour.* Admitting that the trolls 'hit' her 'because they're a little too close to home,' Sabrina went on to say that she has genuine meltdowns for at least ten minutes. But the way she deals with negativity online is taking a step back and saying to herself: 'OK, this isn't real.' The other thing about Sabrina, which shows her compassion and humility the most, is that she doesn't judge the people who have judged her. Instead, she considers that these people may have had something happen to them to make them act this way. 'You have every choice to believe it, or just know and trust who you are. So I try to do that,' she said at the time.

As for being vulnerable in her music, Sabrina is willing to explore her insecurities, emotions and weaknesses. That's what makes a true artist. Especially since the *Emails I Can't Send* days, she shows her fans that there's strength in facing the harder things in life. Although not everyone has the platform that Sabrina has, or the ability to express themselves through song, she notes how important it is to be free and open. Suppressing how you really feel never works out in the end; it always has consequences. Rather, being honest and real with not just her fans but herself is a powerful tool and one that she has mastered after years of self-work and growth.

Back in 2022, when Sabrina was promoting *Emails I Can't Send*, she gave a very open interview to *Vogue*. She explained that, before this album, she'd always been someone who liked to 'change things up', noting how no project she's ever made 'has been the same as the one before'. But the thing she felt was different about her new era at that time was that she'd never been able to write some of her most vulnerable material, which she described as 'more insecure', and 'more forward'. 'I just hadn't felt those emotions,' she admitted.

'I think when you're younger, it's very easy to see the world and think that you can take it on – you have all the confidence required to do that. And then once you start to get humbled by the world, it's very easy to be like, "oh, never mind, backtrack, backtrack."'

During the same interview, Sabrina shared that she even had reservations about being so honest, not because she was scared to open up so much, but because 'it wasn't the fully confident pop record that fans who have been following [her] for a long time might be coming to [her] music for.' Looking back now, Sabrina fans everywhere will feel relieved that she took the initiative and followed her gut instinct.

'I didn't know what to expect, to be honest, but if anything, I realised that there's far more strength in vulnerability and insecurities, because they are the emotions that I think we're all kind of scared to face.'

Like I said, there will always be people waiting behind a computer screen to try to take somebody down. A lot of the time, online trolling is wrapped up in jealousy, insecurity and unhappiness. Sadly, people dealing with such emotions find it hard to be happy for others. Whether they're wrestling with the morality of these negative thoughts or not, this headspace forces them down the rabbit hole of, 'If I'm in a bad place, others deserve to be too.' In contrast, those who are fulfilled in life don't tend to lash out.

But, thankfully, the phrase 'safety in numbers' feels incredibly apt – and empowering – here. Let's unpack:

Sabrina Carpenter isn't the only artist right now embracing such vulnerability. It seems we are currently in the midst of an authentic power movement, and the pop girlies are at the forefront of the campaign.

Yes, I'm talking about the women of the moment, Sabrina (of course), Charli XCX and Chappell Roan. Each have just emerged from the biggest years of their careers, and the overarching theme they projected? Being themselves.

From sensitive lyrics, existential questions and honestly exploring womanhood – from its contradictions to its complexity – each artist released more than just a collection of hits. For the younger millennials and the older Gen Zs, they represent relatability and strength.

The music industry is taking note of this movement too. When was the last time you saw an all-female line-up at a festival that wasn't specifically dedicated to empowering women? Probably not until 2025, when Primavera Sound Festival in Barcelona announced that these three pop queens would be (for want of a better word) running the show. Being messy is hitting the mainstream, girlies!

So, to summarise: Sabrina and Co aren't your run-of-the mill, perfectly polished popstars. They're a new breed of artists who wear their hearts on their sleeves and preach that it's *cool* to be kind. For so long, people have been fed meaningless pop music, written with money and streaming numbers in mind. It doesn't take long for people to work out that what they really crave is realness.

CHAPTER THREE

Short n' Sweet

Short n' Sweet French Martini

Err, because how could I not? Spice (or sweeten) up your next gals' night with the following recipe. I can confirm this mocktail/cocktail is delicious!

3 parts non-alcoholic vodka
1 part raspberry syrup
1 part pineapple juice
Fresh raspberries or a wedge of pineapple, to garnish

1. Firstly, shake all the ingredients, except the garnishes, together in a cocktail shaker with ice.
2. Next, pour the mix into a classic martini glass.
3. Finally, garnish with fresh raspberries or a wedge of pineapple!

Dumb & Poetic

When you're an artist, you have to keep your fans on their toes. In June 2024, while still enjoying the success of 'Espresso', Sabrina announced her sixth studio album, *Short n' Sweet*. She also dropped another monster hit, 'Please Please Please', all within the space of three days.

The song peaked at the top of the *Billboard* Hot 100, becoming Sabrina's first number one single on the chart. It explores relationship insecurities and being scared that your boyfriend could break your heart. Musically, 'Please Please Please' jumps from country pop to synth pop to disco pop, generating comparisons from ABBA to Dolly Parton. It's a demonstration of Sabrina's love for genre-bending. She's always been clear about making music that represents her, and if that means hopping from one sound to another, then that's what she'll do.

The music video for 'Please Please Please' is one that will forever live rent-free in our minds. At the time, Sabrina was dating *Saltburn* star Barry Keoghan, and the pair were very much the Hollywood 'IT' couple. Bearing in mind the themes of the song – in which Sabrina begs her partner not to embarrass her – fans were obsessed with the fact that Barry agreed to be cast as said boyfriend in the video.

During the buzz of the video, Sabrina claimed she was unbiased and had simply cast Barry because she viewed him as 'one of the best actors of this generation'. Sadly, the duo called it quits in December 2024, six months after the video declared them a power couple. The pair cited their busy careers and young ages as the reason for the split.

Despite being number six in the vault, Sabrina has dubbed *Short n' Sweet* as her sophomore album and 'hot older sister' of *Emails I Can't Send.* She considers the latter her debut as a 'fully fledged adult'. In 2024, she told *Variety* that both records were her first shot at having 'full creative control' over a project.

A few familiar names pop up on the album credits, including Julia Michaels, Amy Allen and Steph Jones. A certain someone named Jack Antonoff also made an appearance on the tracklisting, helping to write and produce 'Please Please Please', amongst others. Like I said before, Sabrina had found her A-team, and she had built a creative network she could trust.

As soon as *Short n' Sweet* landed in August 2024, it debuted at number one on the US *Billboard* 200 chart. The feat marked Sabrina's first number one and top 10 album. A month later, the record became platinum-certified after selling one million copies.

Upon its arrival into the world, Sabrina took a few moments to express her gratitude, spiraling over the fact that she was in a position to create such a masterpiece. She penned: '*Short n' Sweet* is officially yours now!!! i feel extremely lucky that each time i write a new record i learn a little bit more about myself, and can create from that place. the making of short n' sweet was one of the most special, honest, up and down, stupid and fun experiences of my life. I thought if something was funny enough to make me laugh then maybe it belonged in a song. happy or sad!'

From 'Espresso' and 'Please Please Please' spawned 'Taste', a campy anthem directed at an ex-boyfriend's new partner, reminding her that Sabrina will always be a part of their relationship. Knowing that the internet literally broke with the Barry x Sabrina collab, this time she wisely called upon another hero: Jenna Ortega. Rightfully dubbed as horror's new scream queen (thanks to her morbid take on Wednesday Addams in the Netflix hit *Wednesday*), Sabrina cast Jenna in the 'Taste' video as the 'girlfriend'. Aesthetically, it was the Gen Z equivalent of Reese Witherspoon and Winona Ryder: Elle Woods vs Lydia Deetz.

But that's as far as that comparison goes. The video is actually an ode to the 1992 fantasy horror film, *Death Becomes Her*, which starred Goldie Hawn and Meryl Streep. Sabrina's story is a love letter to the cult classic, which follows a similar plot of two women who are unable to die – no matter how gory things get. Viewers watch Sabrina and Jenna kill each other over and over again, desperate to get the attention of the same man. Just like the film, 'Taste' ends with the women looking over the grave of the man they both wanted, before laughing and leaving as friends.

Sabrina called the project one of the 'most ambitious videos of [her] life', and noted how Jenna was the only person she had in mind for the character. She shared on Instagram: 'Watching her [Jenna] on screen is a true dream come true and I'm so inspired, impressed, and amazed by her.' Rightfully so, it received the #1 trending video title.

After *Short n' Sweet* dropped, Sabrina broke records in becoming the first female artist in history to achieve the UK's Number 1 album and single simultaneously while dominating all three top positions on the Official Singles Chart with 'Taste' (1), 'Please Please Please' (2) and 'Espresso' (3).

In October, the Official Charts also confirmed that Sabrina was the first artist in 71 years to score '20 weeks at number one on the Official Singles Chart in a year'. By the end of the year, the Charts confirmed that 'Espresso' was the biggest single of 2024 by a female artist.

From viral moments and serving pop culture on a plate, to birthing multiple number ones, it's no surprise that *Short n' Sweet* swept up in terms of award nominations. As well as winning two Grammys at the 2025 show, Sabrina performed at the ceremony.Sabrina opened with a slapstick-comedy jazz version of 'Espresso' wearing a sparkling Old Hollywood-style magician's suit. She delighted the audience with Sabrina-style gags before stripping down to a baby-blue, bejewelled, showgirl bodysuit. After the glittering performance she received a standing ovation from the audience, which included musical greats like Taylor Swift, Beyoncé, Miley Cyrus and Billie Eilish.

At the 2025 BRIT Awards – where she similarly put on quite the show – Sabrina took home one of the most coveted awards of the night: the Global Success Award. Bestowed upon artists who have achieved phenomenal global sales, it's measured by record and concert ticket sales. Since its launch in 2013, Sabrina is the first international artist to scoop the prize.

When thanking her British fans during her acceptance speech, Sabrina joked: 'In a very primarily tea-drinking culture, you streamed the sh*t out of "Espresso".' That's icon energy right there.

As a thank you for *Short n' Sweet*'s Grammy wins, Sabrina once again broke the internet by announcing a deluxe version of the album. Dropping on Valentine's Day, it would feature none other than Dolly Parton on a new version of 'Please Please Please', plus four new tracks: '15 Minutes', 'Couldn't Make It Any Harder', 'Busy Woman' and 'Bad Reviews'

Sabrina also released a music video with Dolly, featuring black-and-white footage of the two driving through Nashville. The new Grammy winner couldn't believe her luck and took to Instagram to share a clip. Alongside the snippet, she wrote: 'Dolly and me singing in a pickup truck!!!!!! I am so honored to have one of my biggest idols on a song that means so much to me. *Short n' Sweet* deluxe is out now! Go watch and listen!!!!'

Elsewhere in the deluxe world, '15 Minutes' went viral on TikTok due to the nature of the lyrics. But before any mums flip out, it's an example of Sabrina's lyrical genius when it comes to dual meanings. What do you mean it's a double entendre about fleeting fame, and not about a guy? Mind = blown

And so this is as far as I can currently go with the Sabrina Carpenter story. As I write, she's halfway through her first arena tour, the *Short n' Sweet Tour*. Never has there been a bigger demand for Sabrina, and never has she deserved all the success she is getting – and more.

‘I never had the plan B, and it wasn’t even a thought in my mind that it wouldn’t work out. I just always knew it was about not if it would happen but when it would happen.’

Please Please Please be Authentically You

By the tender age of 26, Sabrina has achieved things beyond her wildest dreams. While still incredibly young (and with plenty of years of success ahead of her), if you look back to the early days, from interviews to social media posts, she's never lost her humble, appreciative spark. Yes, her hair may have got bigger and blonder, and yes, her songs may not be as innocent as they once were, but deep down, she's still that same young girl from Pennsylvania with huge ambitions and an even bigger heart.

For over 15 years Sabrina persisted through personal and professional hardships, career standstills and uncertainty. But she's always powered through, proving that she's a positive role model worth emulating. Although only standing five feet tall, her reach is stratospheric. Tweens, teens and adults all over the world admire her cheekiness, honesty and ability to pitch herself as the genuine girl next door. She manages to be everybody's best friend – and therapist – all at once. All while running the world as the CEO of pop.

Not to sound cringe, but Sabrina has mastered the recipe for success and modesty. Because if I'm being real for a sec, her world is unrealistic. The majority of us humans will never experience that level of wealth, fame and being so in demand that an entire entourage is required to literally plan our days. Honestly, being the centre of attention 24/7 has the potential to be dangerous, but Sabrina has never succumbed to thinking she is better than anybody else.

It all boils down to the simple dream she's carried with her since she was young: wanting to make people smile, laugh and feel unbounded happiness with the talents that were bestowed upon her. At its core, Sabrina's mission is selfless.

Her journey, marked by resilience, growth, hard work and self-belief, teaches us how important it is to embrace our own authenticity. In the end, staying true to ourselves and finding strength in vulnerability is key.

CHAPTER FOUR

Can't Blame a Girl for Being Inspirational

The Sabrina Effect

After her astronomical success in 2024, the earlier phrase 'The Sabrina Effect' should be added to the Oxford Dictionary. I'd imagine the famous faces I'm about to list would agree, too; hence demonstrating Sabrina's power to inspire those who came, saw and conquered before her.

Firstly, I'd like to introduce Madonna. She's only one of the most iconic, successful and influential pop artists of all time. Plus she's someone Sabrina has admired all her life. When Sabrina revealed her jawdropping, breathtaking, heart-stopping (any other adjectives you can think of) *Vogue* cover in February 2025, the original Material Girl offered up the compliment of all compliments. Sandwiched amongst comments from the likes of Lily Collins, Amelia Dimoldenberg, Marina Diamandis and the official Bratz account, Madonna asked: 'Is this a Valentine's present to me?' Again, not to overuse the word iconic, but the comment sent Sabrina fans into a state of frenzy. A personal favourite response was: 'Madonna did you take the Substance? Tell us.' They were, of course, making a stark reference to the 2024 horror/sci-fi film starring Demi Moore and Margaret Qualley, suggesting that Sabrina was a reincarnation of Madonna.

Secondly, Adele gushed over 'Espresso' during one of her record-breaking Las Vegas residency shows, calling it her 'jam'. Ironically, she joked that it came out when she was on vocal rest so couldn't sing along. But she sure made up for it, telling the crowd: 'So … all last night and this morning, that's what I've been singing. From tomorrow, it'll be "I'm sleeping late, 'cause I'm a singer", because that's what I'm going to do tomorrow.'

Then, when Sabrina covered Shania Twain's 90s' hit, 'That Don't Impress Me Much', the Queen of Country Pop called it a 'huge compliment'. Surely that's all you'd need for life to equal 'made', right?

There are so many reasons Sabrina can be labelled as 'inspirational'. From encouraging her audience to embrace their uniqueness, prioritising their own opinions and values and finding their voice, she shows people that it's OK to be different. You don't have to conform to societal expectations. In her music, she's all about self-discovery and empowerment, while also exploring the heartbreak and melancholy of life. Through song she inspires people to not be afraid to break the mould.

'I am so inspired by so many artists and especially the ones that are constantly changing, growing and pushing the boundaries.'

While it's impossible to single out every musician, Sabrina has regularly cited peers like Taylor Swift and Lorde as her inspirations in the music industry today, both as songwriting influences and in appreciating their work ethics. As for her Netflix Christmas Special, Sabrina made a point to shout out her musical guests. 'It's been such a beautiful gift to be able to celebrate everything that all of these amazing women have done this year. So it was a perfect opportunity to be able to bring some of them together.'

Then, in a full-circle moment, she gushed: 'And Shania Twain! I've looked up to her my whole life. I was so lucky that they volunteered their time. There was a lot of giggles on set.'

'Every feeling that we've ever experienced is beneficial in some way, shape, or form. No feeling is ever useless.'

Sabrina's bad good reviews

'After the Storm' by Kali Uchis – To an R&B pop backing, Kali sings about the personal battles she's faced, while encouraging others to persevere through the tough times. The sun *will* break through the clouds and shine again. Side note: The kitsch music video also feels like something Sabs would have dreamt up.

'Here You Come Again' by Dolly Parton – If you listen to some of the more country-esque tracks on *Short n' Sweet*, the Dolly influence is obvious. The lyrical content in this song also feels similar to some of Sabrina's: an ex-boyfriend charms his way out of purgatory, and his red flags are swiftly thrown in the trash.

'If It Wasn't for the Nights' by ABBA – In true ABBA – and Sabrina – fashion don't be fooled by the relentlessly upbeat disco sounds. Agnetha and Frida are actually wallowing in post-breakup despair.

'*Sarà perché ti amo*' by Ricchi e Poveri – The Italian disco group regularly features on Sabrina's playlists. This track name, which translates to 'It Must Be Because I Love You', is a Miss Carpenter title if ever I've heard one. The string quartet, classic 4/4 pop time signature and cheesy-but-in-a-good-way key change are also classic SC elements.

Sabrina's Pop Icons

Yes, Sabrina's music is unique. She writes about her own experiences, therefore no other artist can theoretically produce a song like her. But if you listen to her records carefully, you can hear doses of musical and lyrical inspiration from a range of icons: Mariah Carey to Britney Spears, Dolly Parton to Aretha Franklin. Regardless of what kind of music you create, every artist will draw influence from other musicians, both past and present. It helps to fuel their own creativity, deepen their understanding of music and explore different avenues of expression.

But what about Sabrina? Let's take a look at the artists who have moved and shaped her into who she is today.

RIHANNA

Musician, actress, businesswoman; Rihanna is the definition of a busy woman. She's one of the best-selling female recording artists of the twenty-first century. Bursting onto the scene in the mid-2000s, Rihanna made an immediate impact on the pop and R&B genres. She's also the recipient of multiple Grammy awards.

What has Sabrina said about Rihanna?

'She's always doing something that we never expect. That's the best thing you can ask for in an artist.'

Debut year: 2005
Spotify listeners per month: 87.8 million+
Studio albums: 8
Grammys won: 9

CHRISTINA AGUILERA

Christina Aguilera is a Grammy-winning artist known for her powerful vocals and hit songs. She is widely heralded as a pop icon. Rising to prominence in the late 90s, she quickly became one of the most celebrated female artists of her era. In the early 2000s, she played a major role in the 'Latin explosion', helping to bring Latin music to a wider audience. Her legacy is long-lasting in the music industry: to this day, she still inspires new generations of artists and fans.

What has Sabrina said about Christina? 'I think the first time I ever heard your voice was [when] my mom played me a video of you singing at eight years old, "A Sunday Kind of Love". That was the most inspiring thing for me ever to see as a young girl that wanted to sing, but just didn't think I could do it at that age.'

Debut year: 1999
Spotify listeners per month: 30.6 million
Studio albums: 9
Grammys won: 5

BRITNEY SPEARS

Like Christina, Britney is a fellow Disney kid, having both come from *The Mickey Mouse Club*. Before the times when it was possible to crash the internet, Britney made headlines in 1998 with '... Baby One More Time'. To this day, people still dress up like the music video for fancy dress parties. Britney is considered a pop legend and is widely recognised as the best-selling teenage artist of all time.

What has Sabrina said about Britney? Sabrina's 2024 VMAs performance paid homage to the 'Oops! ... I Did It Again' music video.

Debut year: 1998
Spotify listeners per month: 40.1 million+
Studio albums: 9
Grammys won: 1

ARETHA FRANKLIN

The 'Queen of Soul' has twice been named by *Rolling Stone* magazine as the greatest singer of all time. Aretha was also the first female performer inducted into the Rock and Roll Hall of Fame. From her unparallelled musical talent, powerful voice and significant contributions to the Civil Rights and feminist movements, Aretha Franklin is a true cultural legend.

What has Sabrina said about Aretha? 'One of the first voices I ever heard as a little girl. My mom played me "Respect" and "Natural Woman", and those songs ... I carried them with me throughout my entire life. I'll show my kids those songs.'

Debut year: 1961
Spotify listeners per month: 10.8 million+
Studio albums: 38
Grammys won: 18

MADONNA

The Queen of Pop. The Material Girl. The Queen of Reinvention. Madonna's decades-long career has been defined by her multifaceted impact on pop culture, music, fashion and feminism. Back in 2010, *Time Magazine* named her one of the most powerful women of the twentieth century. Now we're in the twenty-first century, she's still just as relevant and just as fabulous.

Debut year: 1983
Spotify listeners per month: 38.6 million+
Studio albums: 14
Grammys won: 7

What has Sabrina said about Madonna? Her 2025 *Vogue* cover interview speaks volumes. The whole look *screams* Madonna. Sabrina also wore the pop queen's 1991 Oscars' look to the 2024 MTV Video Music Awards (VMAs). Remember *that* silver-beaded Bob Mackie number? When it comes to Madonna, Sabrina shows her appreciation through fashion.

WHITNEY HOUSTON

Name a more iconic mezzo-soprano voice. We'll wait. Whitney Houston is recognised as one of the most influential R&B artists in history, and is a cultural icon. As well as singing, the late star was also a prolific actor, notably starring in the thriller-romance movie, *The Bodyguard.*

What has Sabrina said about Whitney Houston? Sabrina has always referenced Whitney as an influence.

Debut year: 1985
Spotify listeners per month: 28.7 million+
Studio albums: 7
Grammys won: 6

MARIAH CAREY

No one does the whistle note quite like Mariah. The woman's vocal range is *wild. Rolling Stone* magazine's 'Greatest Singers of All Time' list places her at number five – but we know she's pipped to the post by Sabrina's other idol, Aretha. The outlet also credited Mariah with straddling a 'delicate balance between old-school soul and R&B with modern, often forward-thinking pop'. And how can we forget? She's the Queen of Christmas.

Debut year: 1990
Spotify listeners per month: 27.9 million+
Studio albums: 15
Grammys won: 5

What has Sabrina said about Mariah Carey? While some fans insist Sabrina threw shade at Mariah during her *A Nonsense Christmas* announcement video, I choose to believe she was actually paying homage to her. Dressed in a sparkly Santa bodysuit and fur-trimmed boots, Sabrina nonchalantly asked the camera, 'Expecting someone else?' OK, but how iconic would it have been if Mariah had rocked up for a festive duet??

STEVIE NICKS

One of my personal favourite vocalists – and female musicians of all time – Stevie Nicks sits at the top of the 'coolest women to have ever walked this Earth' list. She's still referred to as the 'Reigning Queen of Rock and Roll', thanks to her work in Fleetwood Mac and her successful solo career. The original boho muse, Stevie's style is witchy and free-spirited: silky shawls, flowy chiffon frocks and 70s high-waisted jeans are staples. Oh, and her smoky, raspy tone. It melts my core every time!

What has Sabrina said about Stevie Nicks? In the past, Sabrina has noted Stevie to be a major inspiration, her unique style helping to shape her own artistic vision.

Debut year: 1973
Spotify listeners per month: 5.9 million+
Studio albums: (solo) 8
Grammys won: 2

DOLLY PARTON

Many millennials were first introduced to 'Aunt Dolly' back in the late naughties during her ad-hoc *Hannah Montana* appearances. Iconic, yes, but Dolly was already a huge star by that point – as I'm sure everybody knows. I mean, she's literally the epitome of country music. Big blonde hair, fringed jackets and hating on the 9–5 aside, Dolly has been an enduring presence in the music industry and cultural zeitgeist for decades. Her strong feminist message and philanthropic work make her a legend.

What has Sabrina said about Dolly Parton? Sabrina has publicly called Dolly an 'icon', and 'idol' and declared that she will 'love her forever'.

Debut year: 1967
Spotify listeners per month: 16 million+
Studio albums: 49
Grammys won: 11

She's also working late, 'cause she's a philanthropist

Sabrina isn't the first celebrity to dip her toes into the world of philanthropy and she won't be the last. But it's always nice when they use their platforms for good.

In 2024, Sabrina followed in their footsteps. She launched The Sabrina Carpenter Fund in partnership with the non-profit PLUS1 as part of her *Short n' Sweet* tour. PLUS1 is a charity focused on supporting social and environmental justice. They partner with celebrities and brands to provide a platform for their initiatives, in the hopes that their reach and impact can go further.

On the launch of her charitable endeavour Sabrina said: 'I am deeply passionate about supporting causes that are close to my heart, including mental health awareness, LGBTQ+ rights and animal welfare. It is incredibly rewarding to see the impact that The Sabrina Carpenter Fund is already making, and I am grateful to my fans for their unwavering support.'

Despite the fund only starting in 2024, many may or may not know that Sabrina has long been involved with charity work. Since 2016 she's been thinking about others and how she can be a positive force in people's lives. As part of her work for the Ryan Seacrest Foundation, a 'non-profit organisation dedicated to inspiring today's youth through entertainment and education focused initiatives', she's flown to hospitals across the US and released charity merchandise.

In 2016 Sabrina recalled an especially heartwarming story from her time working with the foundation. In fact, the exchange was enough to convince her that philanthropy would always be a part of her identity and future. She told *People Magazine* about one 'little girl named Alison' who she visited in a hospital. According to Sabrina, Alison's words were: 'I want to be just like you when I grow up.' When she asked her why, the little girl simply replied: 'Because you're so happy.'

Recalling the event, Sabrina said: 'I think it was so incredible because all those kids are going through so much in their lives – so much more than any of us realise – and they're still so positive. That made me incredibly happy – happier than even she thought I was!'

Fast-forward to the 2025 Grammys, and Chappell Roan made an emotional speech. She told the crowd that if she ever won an award, she'd use it as an opportunity to address 'the most powerful people in music', and demand that 'labels and the industry profiting millions of dollars off of artists would offer a liveable wage and healthcare'. She backed up her plea with cold, hard cash, and donated $25,000 to the US charity Backline, who are 'committed to providing accessible and affordable mental health care options to music industry professionals and their family members'. Chappell then challenged other artists and industry executives to match her donation. Amongst those people who did? Charli XCX, Noah Kahan and, you guessed it, Sabrina.

As part of The Sabrina Carpenter Fund she partnered with PAYPRUS, the prevention of young suicide charity based in the UK. During her *Short n' Sweet* European leg, a percentage of ticket sales from each show went towards supporting charities, including the above. Rainbow Railroad, an organisation that helps at-risk LGBTQ+ people get to safety around the world, also benefitted from the fund.

Other charities that have been helped through The Sabrina Carpenter Fund include:

The Trevor Project: Founded in 1994 by filmmakers Peggy Rajski and Randy Stone, the project provides crisis intervention and suicide prevention services for LGBTQ+ youth.

Pencils of Promise: This charity provides access to education by building schools in underprivileged communities. As of 2025, over 550 schools have been built, and more than 131,000 students in Guatemala, Ghana and Laos have received access to quality education.

Global Citizen: An action platform 'dedicated to achieving the end of extreme poverty'.

According to *Borgen Magazine*, The Sabrina Carpenter Fund had raised over $500,000 as of February 2025. That's no mean feat, considering the organisation had only been running for just eight months at the time. I wonder how much that figure will have increased by the end of the *Short n' Sweet* tour, and how many individuals will have been helped. It's a lovely thought to have.

Taste!

She's really making this easy for me, right? For this cocktail, I thought I'd go full-on Cosmo vibes. Sabrina is a classy gal, after all.

90ml cranberry juice
30ml freshly squeezed lime juice
60ml sparkling water
30ml orange juice

1. Grab a cocktail shaker and add the cranberry juice, lime juice and sparkling water.
2. Add plenty of ice and shake well.
3. Pour into a martini glass.
4. Add a splash of orange juice and, voilà, it's ready to drink!

The Bed Chem

It's true, physics and chemistry both play a significant role in creating the perfect drink. And, as we all know, Sabrina has an old soul. So why not wind down for the evening with a couple of these babies? (Yes, you've guessed it. It's our version of an Old Fashioned!)

Hot water and black tea bags
300g granulated sugar
Aromatic bitters
4 orange peels

1. Steep the tea in a mug of hot water for 3–5 minutes, then let cool.
2. Next, make the simple syrup. Add the granulated sugar and 120ml water to a small saucepan over a medium heat, then stir until the sugar is dissolved. Let it cool, then pour into a jar and seal tightly with a lid.
3. Now the tea and syrup are cool, it's time to create the cocktail! Fill four tumblers with ice (sharing is caring, after all), then to each add 60ml tea, 7ml simple syrup and 2 dashes of bitters.
4. Last but not least, garnish each tumbler with the orange peel.

CHAPTER FIVE

Have TASTE

Although Sabrina's current wardrobe feels very much here to stay, she's always been vocal about how fashion serves as a form of self-expression, and that it's another creative outlet when projecting her persona to the world.

On this note, I urge you to think back to Sabrina's earlier years: her pre-teen pop days were filled with Converse, dungaree dresses and 'girl-next-door' staples. Pardon the pun, but during her *EVOLution* era her style evolved, too. It was out with the sweet, sunshiney vibes and in with the darker, grungier pieces. Teenage angst and all that. Whatever album she was dropping, or whatever aesthetic she was identifying with at the time, Sabrina would embody it through her clothes. In short, no one was telling her what she should wear. She'd never be a clone, and she'd never step out in anything she didn't feel comfortable in or that didn't represented who she was at the time.

What's more, Sabrina knows a strong brand when she sees one. Being consistent with hers through wardrobe, social media, appearances and arena tours contributes a tangible, authentic concept that fans can connect with in a heartbeat.

Fashions fade, style is eternal

Bardot necklines. Rhinestone heart cut-out corsets. Halter bejewelled twinsets. Sheer dresses. Can we all take a moment to gush over Sabrina's wardrobe, please? Ever since her fame snowballed in 2024, she has become a style icon. A fashion muse. An 'IT' girl, whose aesthetic is Old Hollywood glamour

‘I’m a mess if I don’t wear things I feel confident in. Performing is so vulnerable that if you don’t feel 100 per cent good about what you’re in, it’s really hard to do it fearlessly.’

with a modern twist. Pastel colours and vintage silhouettes are non-negotiables, and the higher the platforms, the better.

With that, I imagine everyone has their own favourite Sabrina lookbook. From her *Short n' Sweet* tour catalogue to the fits she wears on the weekend, here's a breakdown of every clothing item, accessory, hair and makeup tip to nail the Sabrina style.

Short n' Sweet tour inspo

Concert dressing is all the rage. As for Sabrina's tour fits, the theme is femininity. Heart and kiss motifs are encouraged (see: required), while baby pink, baby blue and butter yellow are signature colours. Essentially, reflect the album's imagery and overall tone and you're onto a winner.

Platform boots: Sabrina's whole brand is that she's 'short and sweet'. At five feet tall, she plays on her tiny frame and wears items that accentuate her height. Taking inspiration from the Swedish pop pioneers ABBA, Sabrina wears sparkly, just-below-the-knee boots, all of which scream 70s nostalgia.

Sparkly twinsets: To emphasise the 70s' vibes further, stage Sabrina is *obsessed* with the two-piece. Specifically, fitted halterneck tops, diamond in shape and cropped in design.

She pairs these glittery numbers with miniskirts made from the same fabric. I'm *so* here for it.

Catsuit: Other times, it's all about the 1960s' catsuit, complete with a cute 'peddle pusher'-style trouser length. This look is when Sabrina will break away from her pastel colour palette – the slinky black number references the vintage silhouettes from before and really shows off her hourglass figure. The blonde bombshell locks stand out here.

Négligé: Sabrina proves that négligés belong to the beloved naked trend, and when worn with confidence can make the biggest statement of all. You need to be able to see your lace garter, fishnet tights and your favourite Sabrina lyric embroidered onto your thigh.

Corsets: It will always be a performance staple. But not for the reason you think. Singing and dancing on stage for hours on end is a recipe for getting hot and sweaty, so wearing limited clothing actually makes sense. Her corset style relies on Bardot and sweetheart necklines, plenty of jewels, hints of lace and her signature kiss mark.

If you're a *Short n' Sweet* style lover but don't fancy sporting the elaborate pieces on a day-to-day basis, I've got you, too. Allow me to introduce the *Short n' Sweet* tour bus edition:

Any pastel-coloured fit is great: To keep with the vintage theme, grab a pair of capri pants and some cute pumps. Or pop on an oversized baby blue jumper emblazoned with a statement heart on the front. Comfy *and* cool. (Fashion and comfort *can* go hand in hand, you know.)

Sparkles don't have to be on clothes: This could be in the form of hair clips, a skinny Y2K wraparound scarf or a pair of glittery Dr. Martens. Don't forget about the noughties hair glitter, either!

Tulle isn't just for négligés: Whether you don a gathered off-the-shoulder mesh top, a tiered skirt, a sheer ruffled blouse with puffy sleeves, or a French lace-style flared skirt, the naked trend excludes no one. The material is the focus here, as it gives off that cute, flirty feminine energy that's synonymous with Sabrina.

Saturday afternoon Sabrina

Possible scenarios: you've got a day off from touring in Italy, you're wandering the streets of Paris, or London is calling – in any of these, Sabrina has impeccable street style. Or should I say taste? It's far removed from the glitz n' glam of stage life, but still striking and sensual, nevertheless.

Known for her coquette aesthetic – which is characterised by playfulness, romance, femininity and strong 1950s' and 1960s' references – Sabrina's staples include everything from silk ballet flats and little bows, to lace, ruffles and delicate accessories. Whimsical touches are popular, be it tulle dresses and skirts, or vintage floral patterns.

Ready to thrift your way to a Saturday afternoon Sabrina look? Here's everything you'll need:

Milkmaid mini dress: Floral, preferably. And again, pastel colours are a necessity. In terms of a Sabrina must-have, a corset-inspired, scooped or square neckline with a gathered balconette top or tie-front bustier is perfect, along with puff sleeves and perhaps even covered buttons or sweet bows. The mini skirt will be gathered, sometimes with ruffled layers, while lightweight fabrics like cotton or chiffon give the look that elegant, floaty feel.

Babydoll puffball dress: We all know Sabrina loves a puffball skirt – the mini versions, of course. It's all about the fit and flare silhouette here; the fitted bodice makes the skirt that flares out from the waist look even more dramatic.

Mini pleated skirt: Often, Sabrina mixes the coquette aesthetic with Y2K staples, and the mini pleated skirt is a super-cute example of this. Either pale pink, baby blue or earthy tones, make sure you pair the low-rise skirt with a double buckle belt for extra noughties points.

White shirt: While we're on the Y2K vein, every wardrobe needs an oversized, crisp white shirt fitted at the waist. The bigger the collar, the better (we love to make a statement), and the same goes for the cuffs. This item is a dream when worn untucked, with only a couple of buttons done up, and a midi or mini denim skirt. Extra credit for a cute lace bralette underneath.

Lace tights: Depending on the weather, pair these dresses with some white, floral, lace tights.

Ballet pumps: Whatever you wear from this list, a pair of cutesy ballet pumps will complete the look.

Espresso Martinis with Sabrina

Let's set the scene: you've spent the day wrapped in a pink and yellow Stevie Nicks-esque kimono top, a flimsy blue floral mini skirt and a yellow bikini. For the last few hours you've been living your best life, sailing through quaint Italian villages on a small luxe boat, catching those Mediterranean rays. You get back to your hotel and devour a light cheeseboard while listening to your crackly ABBA record, before kicking back with a few of chapters of *Break of Day*, the 1928 novel by the French writer Colette. A while later, you check the clock and it's 6pm, so you google the best rustic bars and restaurants to hit up with your friends later this evening. You know the paparazzi will be there, and as a style icon you need to dress to impress. So, what do you wear?

Sheer dress: Sabrina literally references being in a sheer dress in 'Bed Chem', so it would be rude not to start here. She dons the most *stunning* sheer maxi dress I have ever laid eyes on. Pale blue in colour and made with a thin mesh material, it combines romance with flirtation. Features-wise, look out for a dress with a high-scooped neckline and chunky hemless straps if you want to channel the exact look.

Fitted dress suits: It's giving, 'when you're working 'til 5 but have drinks with the girls at 6'. The fitted dress suit will forever be timeless, and is one of those fundamental pieces that will always save the day if you can't think of what to wear. There

are some key points with this one. The first is that the blazer must always be slightly oversized. The relaxed fit allows for layering and creates a modern, chic silhouette. Secondly, the dress needs to be fitted. Finally, the dress should be the same length as the blazer.

Cut-out satin gowns: This one you reserve for a special occasion – like selling out the entire *Short n' Sweet* tour *and* having 'Espresso' hit number one at Pop Radio. The design goes a little something like this: ultra-high neckline, shoulder-length sleeves, fitted bodice, cut-out on both hips and waist and a flowy maxi skirt that trails slightly behind you. All finished off with a chunky black and gold belt.

Platform heels: Let me first say that platform boots are still welcomed here, just less of the glittery versions. Sabrina has rocked platform *heels* on many occasions, too, often with thin straps and sometimes paired with some cute socks.

A Mountain-dewy Complexion

When you're a famous celebrity you have access to the best in the business. This includes your makeup artist. For Sabrina, her go-to is Carolina Gonzalez, a New York-based makeup artist who is well-versed in celebrity glam.

The woman behind Sabrina's ethereal, doll-like beauty aesthetic doesn't keep her secrets to herself, either. More than once, she's shared her tips and tricks on how to achieve that signature, dewy finish. For one, Carolina hardly uses any powder (yes, I hear you gasp, too – especially at 2am when you've danced yourself into a sweat and your face is glistening for all the wrong reasons). This is because she incorporates skincare into her makeup routine: when your skin is properly hydrated, products won't melt or separate.

She told *E! News* in 2024: 'I like to keep everything moisturised. I barely use powder. I only use it in the T-zone – that is it. When you start getting into powders and start sweating, it will come off. It's like oil and water.' But if you do find yourself in a situation where some of your makeup *has* slipped off, Carolina simply advises you to gently rub, and you're good to go.

Speaking of moisturising, this is how Carolina achieves Sabrina's famous healthy glow: 'I like it to shine. So, I start with the oil-free lotion and then I go on with the serum. Since it's a gel, it's giving you moisture but it's not going to make your stuff crack.' The products she's talking about? Cetaphil's Oil-Free Hydrating Lotion and Healthy Renew Eye Gel Serum. Both are accessible to regular folk like us, as they won't break the bank.

Sabrina's glowy complexion is complimented by further defining features: vixen eyes with fluffy lashes and pouty lips. Many times the latter screams Y2K, thanks to overlined lipliner that's slightly darker in shade than the gloss on the actual lips. For those of us who grew up with Bratz dolls, think a subtler, less-intense version.

Last but not least, no Sabrina makeup routine is complete without a whole load of blush. Like her honey-blonde locks, rosy cheeks are synonymous with the overall 'Sabrina Carpenter' look. Out of all the steps, it's probably the one that gives the most classic vintage vibes.

Lucky for blush-lovers everywhere, we've got a free demo, too. Carolina shared: 'I always start lightly. You never want to go in too heavy. With Sabrina, placement is also key. I love to give her a doll look, and so the blush takes the place of highlight because it lifts the face. Blush is the new highlight for me.' Err, sold.

For the weekends: Looking for a little extra 'something' to complete your beauty look? Sabrina is partial to another Y2K staple: body glitter. But don't go OTT with it, the last thing you want to do is look like you're going to your primary school disco. Instead, lightly dab your collarbones and chest with roll-on body glitter – just enough so that it glistens when the light hits you.

To béret or not to béret?

The answer is *always.* An outfit is never complete without accessories. Here are just a few items Sabrina has sported in her time:

Hair bow: The peak coquette accessory! To match Sabrina, wear your hair in a half-up half-down do, with your bangs loose out front to frame your face.

Ribbon: Because it's romantic.

Neck tie: To feel like you're the main character in an Audrey Hepburn film.

Pile on the necklaces, stack those rings: We love a charm necklace, a 'short n' sweet' pendant, or if you're feeling glam, layers of diamond jewellery.

Shoulder bag: You've got to have somewhere to store your favourite sunnies and digital camera, right?

Satin headband: For when you're driving through Nashville in a pickup truck with Dolly Parton.

Bandana: Make sure it's the same material as the dress for major holiday vibes.

Knee-high socks: Preppy and playful, these will look great with a bubble skirt, fitted polo top and platform heels.

Béret: No reason other than it's chic x 1000.

Feather Your Feminism

Let it be known that, rather than advocating for a specific political ideology, Sabrina's feminism represents and emphasises individual empowerment and authenticity. She believes that the diversity of perspectives is one of the keys to achieving progress.

Despite her positive outlook on life, she's not dodged the 'regressive' comments about her sexuality. It's a shame. In my opinion – and I know many others agree – I love to see a bold, confident woman owning her character and projecting the narrative that it's OK to be yourself. Heck, we encourage it.

Thankfully, Sabrina is so self-assured these days that she's not letting such opinions get to her. Instead, she's using her platform to get her message across. Loud and proud.

'My message has always been clear – if you can't handle a girl who is confident in her own sexuality, then don't come to my shows,' she stated. 'Female artists have been shamed forever. In the noughties it was Rihanna, in the nineties it was Britney Spears, in the eighties it was Madonna – and now it's me.'

It's true. Rihanna was a victim in 2017 when a blogger accused her of 'rocking some new high key thickness'. And 2017 wasn't even that long ago. You'd think that being in such a body-positive era, problematic comments like this – that are so glaringly obvious – would cease to exist. Unfortunately, there is still so much work to be done.

As for Britney, she was called a 'whale' in 2007. Yes, really. She called out the hateful comments in her track 'Piece of Me', where she noted that whatever her size, she'll never look 'right'. As a millennial, it's hard to believe the level of body-shaming that went on – and was accepted – in the early 2000s. I want to scream.

Madonna? In the 80s, she was slut-shamed by the Catholic Church. I'll leave that there.

Sabrina delved into this issue further with *The Sun*. She expressed her frustration of critics ignoring talent in favour of spreading vitriol.

'It's essentially saying that female performers should not be able to embrace their sexuality in their lyrics, in the way we dress, in the way we perform. It is totally regressive. It's like those who want to shame don't make comments when I talk about self-care or body positivity or heartbreak, which are all normal things a 25-year-old goes through. They just want to talk about the sexual side of my performances.'

Unfortunately, the double standards between male and female artists have existed for years. Think about it. When Harry Styles went solo and started dressing with an androgynous edge, it was celebrated. His gender-fluid wardrobe (take his 2019 Met Gala look, consisting of a sheer, frilled, black blouse and tailored trousers, or his David Bowie-inspired *Love on Tour* flared jumpsuits) are examples of this. Rather than being ridiculed for ditching the stereotypical fashion choices of a cis man, critics applauded him for challenging traditional gender norms through his style. He's now considered a fashion icon.

Speaking of David Bowie, his fashion legacy made a revolutionary cultural impact, which has since paved the way for more experimental trends. Embracing unconventional items and silhouettes, bold colours, sequins and makeup, he created looks that were provocative and playful. (Does that sound like someone we know?) He pushed boundaries and was rewarded by designers who took his influence to the runway.

As for lyricism, Marvin Gaye's 'Sexual Healing' is one of the most beloved songs to exist. Despite directly addressing sexual themes, the soul icon was praised for his sensual and emotional approach. His prize? The song has been ranked high on *Rolling Stone's* 500 Greatest Songs of All Time, plus other 'best of' lists.

Of course, I'm not here to tear down the accomplishments of these artists, nor others who came before or after. I'm simply asking why, when male artists express their sexuality, show a bit of skin and generally play into the 'sex sells' market, are they not shamed? Like Sabrina has asked, why is it one rule for them, and another for us?

Having first-hand experience of such shaming has been a catalyst for Sabrina's 'women supporting women' mantra. She said: 'As women, we can look at another woman and be like, "Oh, she has the perfect body," But if you were to ask the woman you think has a perfect body, I guarantee she will have her own insecurities. That's why as women we need to be kind to each other.'

With that, here are a few tips on how you can spread positivity. The more you take up space with the 'good', the less room there is for the 'bad'. It's that simple.

Compliment: What's better than receiving a heartfelt compliment, especially if you're having a bad day? I'll wait. It boosts morale, fosters positivity, strengthens relationships, enhances moods and increases confidence.

Use social media for good: The power of social media is immense. Wherever you can, be an ally. Share encouraging quotes, important resources and uplifting articles. Reply to your friends' stories with hearts and loving messages. Let people know you're here for them.

Random acts of kindness: Whether it's holding a door open for a stranger, forwarding a supportive message to a friend or picking up a coffee for a colleague, small, kind acts can have a huge positive impact on someone's day.

'If you don't have anything nice to say, don't say it at all. And if you do have to say it, make it really funny so I can screenshot it and save it for later.'

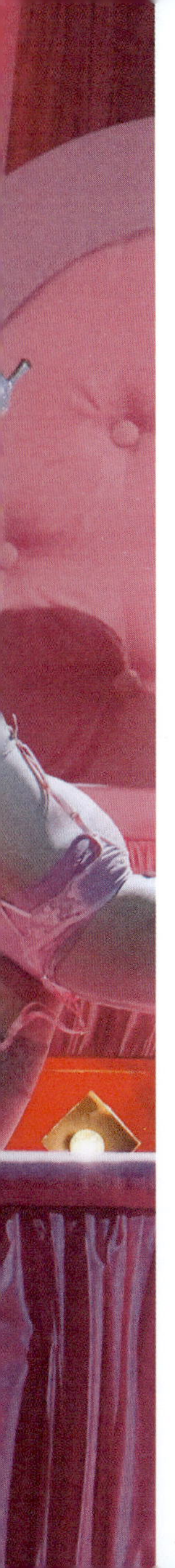

CHAPTER SIX

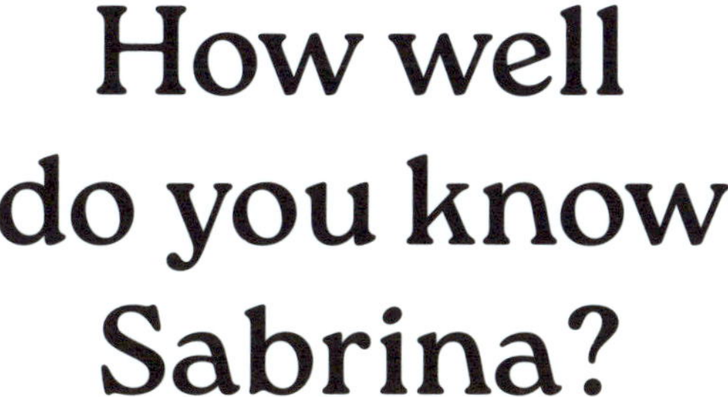

How well do you know Sabrina?

Earlier on, you found out how Sabrina you are. Now it's time to find out how well you know Sabrina. From her humble beginnings in Pennsylvania to her current status as a global pop icon, no stone will be left unturned here. So, Carpenters, rack those brains, whip out your pink fuzzy ... pens, and prepare for some serious pop girlie trivia. Welcome to the Sabrina pop quiz, it won't take more than 15 minutes.

1. What is Sabrina Carpenter's middle name?

a. Annabel
b. Annlynn
c. Alison

2. What was Sabrina Carpenter's first acting role?

a. Orange is the New Black
b. The Goodwin Games
c. Law & Order: Special Victims Unit

3. What Grammys did Sabrina Carpenter win at the 2025 awards?

a. Album of the Year and Best New Artist
b. Record of the Year and Song of the Year
c. Pop Vocal Album and Pop Solo Performance

4. What is Sabrina Carpenter's date of birth?

a. 11 May 1999

b. 18 August 1998

c. 2 December 1996

5. What was Sabrina Carpenter's first number one?

a. 'Espresso'

b. 'Please Please Please'

c. 'Taste'

6. Which Broadway musical did Sabrina Carpenter star in?

a. Mean Girls

b. West Side Story

c. Chicago

7. What are the names of Sabrina Carpenter's sisters?

a. Summer, Sophie and Sienna

b. Lily, Laura and Lizzie

c. Carly, Sarah and Shannon

8. What town is Sabrina Carpenter from?

a. Quakertown

b. Pittsburgh

c. West Chester

9. In which song does Sabrina Carpenter sing about a cute boy who wears a white jacket?

a. 'Bed Chem'
b. 'Juno'
c. 'Coincidence'

10. How old was Sabrina Carpenter when she signed with Hollywood Records?

a. 10
b. 11
c. 12

11. What year did Sabrina Carpenter sign with Island Records?

a. 2019
b. 2020
c. 2021

12. What Taylor Swift songs did Sabrina Carpenter perform with Taylor at the *Eras Tour*?

a. 'White Horse', 'Coney Island' and 'Is It Over Now?'
b. 'Picture to Burn', 'Love Story' and 'Lavender Haze'
c. 'You Belong With Me', 'Marjorie' and 'Dear John'

13. What was Sabrina Carpenter's Netflix Christmas Special called?

a. Christmas with the Carpenters
b. A Nonsense Christmas with Sabrina Carpenter
c. Sabrina Carpenter's Jingle Bell Ball

14. Which artists did Sabrina Carpenter perform with during her Christmas Special?

a. Tyla, Shania Twain, Kali Uchis and Chappell Roan
b. Taylor Swift, Raye, Suki Waterhouse and Kylie Minogue
c. Dolly Parton, Christina Aguilera, Adele and Stevie Nicks

15. What video game did Sabrina Carpenter collaborate with in 2025?

a. Minecraft
b. Fortnite
c. The Sims

16. What award did Sabrina Carpenter win at the 2025 Brit Awards?

a. Best New Artist
b. Album of the Year
c. Global Success Award

17. Who did Sabrina Carpenter support on tour in 2017?

a. Ariana Grande

b. Lady Gaga

c. Katy Perry

18. Which actress starred in the 'Taste' video?

a. Millie Bobby Brown

b. Zendaya

c. Jenna Ortega

19. What was Sabrina Carpenter's most-streamed song of 2024?

a. 'Please Please Please'

b. 'Feather'

c. 'Espresso'

20. Who was the celebrity host for Sabrina Carpenter's first *Saturday Night Live* musical guest appearance?

a. Jake Gyllenhaal

b. Timothée Chalamet

c. Mikey Madison

Sabrina
Carpenter,
a love letter

There's never a dull moment in Sabrina Carpenter's universe.

One night she's arresting Salma Hayek with fuzzy pink handcuffs, the next she's ad-libbing witty, and often NSFW, outros to her songs. Of course, all of this camaraderie (every pun intended) is done exuding Hollywood blonde-bombshell realness, in custom Victoria's Secret corsets.

Put simply? Whatever fun, campy or playful stunt Sabrina Carpenter pulls, it will *always* be iconic, and it will *always* break the internet.

Sabrina is quite literally the definition of short and sweet. During her March 2025 *Vogue* cover interview, the 26-year-old admitted that the title of her sixth studio album isn't a created character but an exaggerated, theatrical version of herself. '*Short n' Sweet* is absolutely me. There's no, like, alter ego,' she mused.

And that's exactly why we love her. She's real. She's honest. She's raw. And perhaps our favourite, she doesn't take herself too seriously. Life is short, so we might as well make it sweet, after all.

But even though 2024 was a year of huge successes for Sabrina; from joining The Beatles as the only acts ever to simultaneously chart their first three top 5 hits on the *Billboard* Hot 100, to becoming the first female artist to hold the number one and number two spots on the UK singles chart for three weeks in a row, let's not forget the years of hard work she's put into her craft. (Side note: imagine dethroning yourself in the charts. It's quite legendary, really.)

Like fellow pop icons such as Chappell Roan and Charli XCX, Sabrina has been on the scene for a long time, honing her skills, building her fanbase and figuring out who she is as an artist. Although it's hard to remember, Sabrina was once a 13-year-old girl thrown into the showbiz world when she booked *Girl Meets World*, a reboot of the classic 90s series *Boy Meets World.*

Despite having huge talents and big dreams, it's taken over a decade for Sabrina to reach 'icon' status. It's something that, now in her mid-20s, she's content with. She told *Time Magazine* in October 2024 that recent bucket-list moments (from hosting *SNL* to performing at the VMAs) were things she wanted to achieve earlier in her career. But in retrospect, looking at how things have unfolded, she now feels grateful for the longer journey. After all, there's nothing wrong with being a late bloomer. Our dreams will come true when the time is right, and we'll be ready for it. Sabrina said: 'I feel so prepared for these moments. If I was even 17 or 18, I think I would have been way, way more nervous and intimidated.'

And during the interview, it's almost as if she manifested what was to follow. Speaking about the next career goal guaranteed to make her scream, cry and throw up, it was all about performing at the Grammys. The two awards she won at the 2025 ceremony (Pop Vocal Album for *Short n' Sweet* and Pop Solo Performance for 'Espresso') must have been the cherry on top of an already very sweet cake.

So, while some of you may have joined the fandom during her stint at the *Eras Tour* or following Sabrina's summer when

'Espresso' and 'Please Please Please' were inescapable, others have been there since the very beginning. But the commonality we all share? We love her just the same.

From the Disney days to the Grammy-winning star we now see before us, let's raise a limoncello spritz to the queen of sarcasm, sharp wit, cheeky pop hits and the coquette aesthetic.

Quiz Answers

So, how well did you do? All the answers are below. No cheating!

1) Annlynn
2) *Law & Order: Special Victims Unit*
3) Pop Vocal Album and Pop Solo Performance
4) 11 May 1999
5) 'Please Please Please'
6) *Mean Girls*
7) Carly, Sarah and Shannon
8) Quakertown
9) 'Bed Chem'
10) 12
11) 2021
12) 'White Horse', 'Coney Island' and 'Is It Over Now?'
13) *A Nonsense Christmas with Sabrina Carpenter*
14) Tyla, Shania Twain, Kali Uchis and Chappell Roan
15) *Fortnite*
16) Global Success Award
17) Ariana Grande
18) Jenna Ortega
19) 'Espresso'
20) Jake Gyllenhaal

References

Aguirre, A. 'How the World Fell for Sabrina Carpenter', *Vogue,* 2025 (www.vogue.com/article/sabrina-carpenter-march-cover-2025-interview)

Allaire, C. 'Sabrina Carpenter Talks Her New Versace Campaign, Performing With Chappell Roan & What Made Her Spotify Wrapped', *Vogue,* 2024 (www.vogue.co.uk/article/sabrina-carpenter-christmas-special-interview)

Aramesh, W. 'Sabrina Carpenter gave us the song of the summer. She's got a plan for all seasons', *Rolling Stone,* 2024 (https://au.rollingstone.com/music/music-features/sabrina-carpenter-espresso-short-n-sweet-taylor-swift-interview-61709/)

Aswad, J. 'Sabrina Carpenter Signs With Island Records', *Variety*, 2021 (https://variety.com/2021/music/news/sabrina-carpenter-signs-island-records-1234891659/)

Baldsing, J. 'Sabrina Carpenter comes into her own on Singular: Act I', *The Line Of Best Fit*, 2018 (www.thelineofbestfit.com/reviews/albums/sabrina-carpenter-singular-act-i-album-review)

Bardsley, M. 'Hitmakers: The songwriting secrets behind Sabrina Carpenter's Espresso', *Music Week,* 2024 (www.musicweek.com/interviews/read/hitmakers-the-songwriting-secrets-behind-sabrina-carpenter-s-espresso/090901)

Campbell, E. 'Sabrina Carpenter, Superstar', *Paper Magazine,* 2024 (/www.papermag.com/sabrina-carpenter-cover)

Cartwright, S. 'Sabrina Carpenter On Finding Her Light During Really Dark Times', *Stylecaster,* 2022 (https://stylecaster.com/entertainment/celebrity-news/1257666/sabrina-carpenter/)

Casteel, B. 'Sabrina Carpenter tackles overthinking in new track "In My Bed"', *Substream Magazine,* 2019 (https://substreammagazine.com/2019/06/sabrina-carpenter-in-my-bed/)

Craig, N. 'Sabrina Carpenter Releases "In My Bed" Music Video', *Celeb Mix*, 2019 (https://celebmix.com/sabrina-carpenter-releases-in-my-bed-music-video/)

Cubit, B. 'Sabrina Carpenter on Filming The Short History of the Long Road, Writing Music, and More', *Pop Sugar*, 2020 (www.popsugar.com/entertainment/sabrina-carpenter-last-call-interview-47554755)

Dodson P. Claire, 'Sabrina Carpenter on Her Career, from "Girl Meets World" to "Work It"', *Teen* Vogue, 2020 (www.teenvogue.com/story/sabrina-carpenter-girl-meets-world-to-work-it)

D'Souza, S. ''I'm a tyrant!' Pop superstar Sabrina Carpenter on freakish fame, fighting Disney and writing the song of the summer', *Guardian*, 2024 (www.theguardian.com/music/article/2024/aug/23/im-a-tyrant-pop-superstar-sabrina-carpenter-on-freakish-fame-fighting-disney-and-writing-the-song-of-the-summer)

Epstein, R. 'Sabrina Carpenter Is Ready for Act II', *Marie Claire*, 2019 (https://www.marieclaire.com/celebrity/a28184345/sabrina-carpenter-interview-2019/)

Feldman, L. 'Sabrina Carpenter Has Waited Her Whole Life for This', *Time Magazine,* 2024 (https://time.com/7027418/sabrina-carpenter-interview-time-100-next/)

@sabrinacarpenter, Instagram, 23 March 2024

Frank Reeves, M. 'Sabrina Carpenter on *The Eras Tour* and dating in the public eye', *Cosmopolitan UK,* 2024 (https://sabrina-carpenter.com/2024/05/27/1515/)

Garcia, T. 'Summer of Sabrina Carpenter: Hitting No. 1 on the Charts, Getting Advice From Best Friend Taylor Swift and What Barry Keoghan Really Thinks About Her Lyrics', *Variety,* 2024 (https://au.variety.com/2024/music/features/sabrina-carpenter-talks-top-charts-taylor-swift-barry-keoghan-16803/)

Goldfield Rodrigues, B, 'Track By Track Review Of EVOLution By Sabrina Carpenter', *ANDPOP*, 2016 (https://web.archive.org/web/20161109085407/http://www.andpop.com/2016/10/14/track-track-review-evolution-sabrina-carpenter/)

Goldsztajn, I. '24 Hours With Sabrina Carpenter', *Marie Claire*, 2022 (https://www.marieclaire.com/beauty/sabrina-carpenter-beauty-routine/)

Hess, L. 'Sabrina Carpenter On The Radical Honesty Of Her New Album, *Emails I Can't Send*', *Vogue,* 2022 (https://www.vogue.co.uk/arts-and-lifestyle/article/sabrina-carpenter-interview-emails-i-cant-send)

Huber, E. 'Becoming a Pop Star Was Sabrina Carpenter's Destiny', *Who What Wear*, 2023 (https://www.whowhatwear.com/uk/sabrina-carpenter-interview)

Jones, D. 'Sabrina Carpenter hits out at Stock, Aitken & Waterman's "regressive" comments: "If you can't handle it, don't come to my shows,"' *NME*, 2025 (https://www.nme.com/news/music/sabrina-carpenter-hits-out-at-stock-aitken-watermans-regressive-comments-if-you-cant-handle-it-dont-come-to-my-shows-3832060)

M. Sellers, C. 'Album Review: Sabrina Carpenter's *EVOLution*', *The Celebrity Cafe*, 2016 (https://thecelebritycafe.com/2016/10/201610album-review-sabrina-carpenters-evolution/amp/)

Manson, A. 'V Girls: Sabrina Carpenter', *V Magazine*, 2023 (https://vmagazine.com/article/v-girls-sabrina-carpenter/)

McCarthy, L. 'Sabrina Carpenter Is Making the Leap With Her New Album, Singular: *Act 1*', *W Magazine*, 2018 (www.wmagazine.com/story/sabrina-carpenter-album-singular-act-1)

Morin, A. 'Here's How to Keep Makeup Sweatproof Without Powder, According to Sabrina Carpenter's Makeup Artist', *E! News*, 2024 (www.eonline.com/news/1401498/sabrina-carpenters-makeup-artist-reveals-why-powder-doesnt-keep-makeup-sweatproof)

@plus1org, Instagram, 13 August 2024

Rearick, L. 'Sabrina Carpenter takes us inside her most confessional song yet', *Hollywood Records*, 2019 (www.hollywoodrecords.com/app/uploads/2019/05/Sabrina-Carpenter.pdf)

Rix, Lucy. 'Sabrina Carpenter on growing up, lie changing events and the future', *Student Pocket Guide*, 2019 (www.thestudentpocketguide.com/2018/06/entertainment/music/sabrina-carpenter-interview-growing/)

Runtagh, J. 'Sabrina Carpenter Reveals How Helping Out with the Ryan Seacrest Foundation Inspired Her', *People*, 2016 (www.yahoo.com/entertainment/sabrina-carpenter-reveals-helping-ryan-223009888.html)

@sabrinacarpenter, Instagram, 24 August 2024

@sabrinacarpenter, Instagram, 14 February 2025

'Sabrina Carpenter Creates the Playlist to Her Life', *Teen Vogue*, 2018 (www.youtube.com/watch?v=5NahQrslgQ4)

Sabrina Carpenter interview, *VMAs red carpet* (2018)

Smith, K. Louise 'Sabrina Carpenter calls out mothers who criticise her "risqué" Short n' Sweet tour outfits',

Capital FM, 2024 (www.capitalfm.com/news/sabrina-carpenter-met-gala-louis-vuitton-pharell-pants/)

Waheed, J. 'Sabrina Carpenter on navigating her twenties, finding her voice through music and "adding to her story" with *Emails I Can't Send* deluxe edition', *Glamour*, 2023 (www.glamourmagazine.co.uk/article/sabrina-carpenter-interview-2023)

Wetmore, B. 'Sabrina Carpenter's Next Act', *Paper Magazine*, 2019 (www.papermag.com/sabrina-carpenter-singular-act2)

Whittum, C. 'Sabrina Carpenter on Her Mature New Album and Treadmill-Ready Single "Almost Love"', *Billboard*, 2018 (https://www.billboard.com/music/music-news/sabrina-carpenter-almost-love-interview-new-album-singular-8461765/)

Picture Credits

pp2–3: Max Cisotti/Dave Benett/Getty Images
pp4–5: Kevin Mazur/Getty Images for AEG
pp12–13: Charles Sykes/Invision/Associated Press/Alamy Stock Photo
p21: Steve Jennings/WireImage/Getty Images
pp38–39: Michael Tran/AFP via Getty Images
p43: WENN Rights Ltd/Alamy Stock Photo
p55: Roberto Ricciuti/Redferns/Getty Images
p69: Max Cisotti/Dave Benett/Getty Images
p73: Image Press Agency/Alamy Live News
pp78–79: Christopher Polk/Rolling Stone via Getty Images
p84: Gareth Cattermole/Getty Images
p89: Jim Dyson/Getty Images
pp90–91: Richard Shotwell/Invision/AP/Alamy Stock Photo
p106: Kevin Mazur/Getty Images for AEG
pp108–109: Chris Pizzello/Associated Press/Alamy Stock Photo
p119: John Nacion/NurPhoto SRL/Alamy Stock Photo
p123: Kristy Sparow/Getty Images for Vogue
pp128–129: PA Images/Alamy Stock Photo
p135: Michael Stewart/INSTARimages.com/Alamy Stock Photo

All illustrative elements: Shutterstock.com

HarperCollins*Publishers*
1 London Bridge Street
London SE1 9GF

www.harpercollins.co.uk

HarperCollins*Publishers*
Macken House, 39/40 Mayor Street Upper
Dublin 1, D01 C9W8, Ireland

First published by HarperCollins*Publishers* 2025

10 9 8 7 6 5 4 3 2 1

A catalogue record of this book is available from the British Library

ISBN 978-0-00-878111-8

Printed and bound by PNB Print, Latvia

This book is produced from FSC™ certified paper and other controlled sources to ensure responsible forest management.

For more information visit: www.harpercollins.co.uk/green